A Community of Love

The family is a community of love
where every member feels understood, accepted and loved
and seeks to understand, accept and love the others.

—John Paul II

A Community of Love

SPIRITUALITY OF FAMILY LIFE

David M. Thomas

A COMMUNITY OF LOVE
Spirituality of Family Life
by David M. Thomas

Edited by Marcia Broucek
Cover design by Thomas A. Wright
Design and typesetting by Patricia A. Lynch
Images from *Family Album* and *Family Album II* by Michael Fleishman.

All quotes from Pope John Paul II are from *Familiaris Consortio (On the Family)*. Quote from Pope Paul VI is from *Evangelii Nuntiandi (Evangelization in the Modern World)*.

Published by ACTA Publications, 5559 W. Howard Street, Skokie, IL 60077
(800) 397-2282 www.actapublications.com.

Library of Congress Number: 2006935396
ISBN 10: 0-87946-327-9
ISBN 13: 978-0-87946-327-4
Printed in the United States of America
Year: 15 14 13 12 10 9 8 7
Printing: 10 9 8 7 6 5 4 3 2 1

I dedicate these pages to the many students who have been given to me for over forty years of teaching. I can think of no other greater sacred calling, nor one with as many blessings, as that of a teacher. I want to include in my dedication their families too. As I state in the pages that follow, we are never alone. We journey through our days and nights with others, often with our families, both present and past. And in the midst of it all, God is also there, not as a passive observer but as One who dwells with us, whether we are conscious of it or not. One of my goals in *A Community of Love* is to open our eyes to God's hidden presence, where life and love meet, ignite and create anew, day after day.

We need to talk....

Family life has changed dramatically over the last century, and I am not impressed by how our culture supports family life today. Society pays too little attention to the survival of the family, and government seems open to providing only token assistance. Corporations and other large enterprises treat family as a necessary problem. Mass media treats family like Play-Doh, shaping it to whatever odd shape or size the media needs to hawk its products.

The challenges of family living can easily compete with any of life's other trials and tribulations. M. Scott Peck's most quoted line in his monumental bestseller, *The Road Less Traveled*, states, "Life is difficult." You might recall that he wrote it somewhat as a response to what he viewed as the free and easy approach to life that seemed to be part of the sixties and seventies. In a later work called *Further Along the Road Less Traveled,* he added that life is also complex, addressing those who seemed bent on reducing the rigors of daily living to simple formulas or solutions.

He was right on both counts. Life is difficult and complex. And when you apply these characteristics to family life, you can add superlatives to the description.

Some think the family as an institution is in its final days. Or that it is replaceable by some other social arrangement. However, while it is true that many challenges assault families today, I cannot agree.

Even amid the pervasive depersonalizing forces of today, many families do stay together. In fact, as unconventional as this may sound, I wonder whether many families might be better today than ever. They embody mutual respect and a healthy regard for the goodness of each family member, and their love for one another seems boundless. They also stand in service to the needs of others outside the family.

But I must also add—both from my experience and my research—that not a single one of them made it to where they are without hard work and a few tears. Families can look pretty battle worn at times, but like warriors returning from battle, their cuts, bruises and scars can be badges of courage and commitment.

Their effort seems to be come more from within than from the surrounding culture, but fortunately a few organizations—mostly grassroots groups—commit both time and effort to support family life. Perhaps the only large institution on record trying to help families is organized religion. Churches, synagogues and mosques have all expressed solid support of the family. But religious groups today sometimes seem so embroiled in their own struggle for survival that they have little energy left for other groups. So when churches try to partner with the family, they may appear like two wounded wayfarers leaning on each other as they walk slowly along the path.

In the autumn of 1980, I found myself overseas for the first time in my life. I had been invited to serve as a peritus (expert advisor) to the United States bishops who were participating in the first international synod at the Vatican called by Pope John Paul II. The topic under discussion was the role of the Christian family in the modern world.

Families can look pretty battle worn at times, but like warriors returning from battle, their cuts, bruises and scars can be badges of courage and commitment.

John Paul II wrote more about the role of the family in both church and society than any other pope in history. Perhaps his own family grief—losing a baby sister, then his mother at an early age; later, his older brother and his father, all before he was ordained as a priest—was part of the late pope's consistent and compelling support of family life. He affirmed the importance of the family, and proclaimed over and over again that the community of family was an irreplaceable source of life for both the church and society. Because family life brings to many their deepest joy as well as their most trying moments, he included family as one of the "essentials" for the life of the human person.

One of John Paul II's greatest contributions was his ability to connect the seemingly secular, such as family life, with the outpouring of God's life and love into creation. He was especially adept at making this connection when it came to the more difficult and challenging aspects of life, including the difficulties inherent in family life. I am grateful for his many insights into the spiritual life of the family, and my wife and I have applied his teachings in the *Familiaris Consortio (On the Family)* to our own family.

Over the years, I have taught on the theological and spiritual dimensions of marriage and family life, and written widely on the topic. I have also been called to advise and write for the Catholic bishops of the United States in matters dealing with sexuality, marriage and family life. But before I go any further, you need to know that I am no abstract idealist, no airy theologian when it comes to family life. I know from experience the difficult moments and hard edges of family life. But I also know its moments of delight and satisfaction.

My "first family," the family I was born into, was a Catholic family in Hammond, Indiana. All my grandparents were immigrants to the United States, my father's parents coming from Lithuania and my mother's parents from Germany. I was the eldest, the only son with three sisters. My strongest memories of growing up are filled with the presence of aunts, uncles and cousins. We lived in close proximity to each other, and when we combined both parents' families, we numbered around fifty. Each holiday brought a large group together for loud, boisterous and playful times. I also recall many heated arguments, which mostly ended with smiles all around.

I think of my "second family" as the religious community I entered when I was eighteen years old. One of the reasons I wanted to become a Holy Cross religious was that part of their mission was to develop "community spirit" among its members. But as I neared the time for my ordination to the priesthood, important questions surfaced both for the community and myself whether I had chosen the right path for me. Eventually, through difficult and sometimes painful reflection, I came to realize that I was being called elsewhere. So a little shy of forty years ago, I walked out the door of the seminary. I was twenty-six years old and ready to start anew. But I had grown a thousand ways during those years with a wonderful group of young men, many of whom have remained lifelong friends.

My "third family" began with my marriage to Karen. The date of our wedding was 6/11/66, which, if it were a poker hand, would mean a full house. My third family became exactly that. We eventually numbered seven: one daughter, the eldest, and four sons. When our youngest son was five years old, we began to take in foster children, most of whom were infants. Over the next twenty years, we experienced all the joys and sufferings that came with caring for over seventy little ones, many of whom were labeled "special needs" children. This meant that they came to us with serious physical or emotional needs. When asked if this was very difficult, I would usually mention that in a home full of adolescents—which our home was—it was wonderful. When our teenage children complained that they had it hard, we would need only to remind them of these little ones' difficulties and their complaints would evaporate.

My wife and I were getting close to our autumn years, and we began to talk about pulling back from foster parenting and turning our attention more to grandchildren. We were beginning to feel a bit tired, and it seemed time to move on. Then one day the phone rang. It was a social worker with whom we had worked to place one of our foster children just a few months earlier. Her words were like a lighting bolt directly striking our home: "They don't want her anymore." She referred to a little girl we had cared for from her earliest days until she was two. A new era of family life for us was about to begin.

We were stunned. How could anyone not want this precious little girl? But we also were familiar enough with the world of foster care and adoption to know that abandonment happens—more often than the general public is aware of.

Our immediate response was to request that she be returned to us as a foster child until a new family could be found to adopt her. There was a silent pause on the phone.

"We can't do that," replied the worker. "It would be too hard on her to have to leave you again. Unless you would keep her."

Adoption? A decision we had never considered for ourselves. If you were committed to foster care, as we were, it was almost a form of suicide to think of ever adopting any of the little ones you cared for. We loved them all as our own while they were with us. We knew our role and were accepting of both its joys and its pain. But we just never considered keeping any of our family visitors. Until then.

For a decision of this magnitude, my wife and I felt we needed some outside help. Fortunately, we found a wonderful therapist who had been working with adoptions for fifty years. We needed clarity, and we needed to face all the practicalities involved, should we choose to adopt. I was almost sixty, and my wife was not far behind. That's grandparent age, not a time to begin parenting again.

After three weeks of considered conversation, we decided to adopt a new little daughter. We called social services and arranged a time for "pick up." I must say that, as we drove to the agency, my stomach had more butterflies in it than I had on my wedding day.

Our new daughter's "things" were stacked in a pile outside the door. I carefully picked up each item—a small bike, a doll stroller, an assorted menagerie of stuffed animals and a blanket—all items we had given her before she had left us for her new home.

Then we were escorted to an empty room to await her arrival. Finally, after what seemed hours, the door opened and out the little angel walked. She was three years old. Surely there could not be any greater abundance of joy than when my wife wrapped her arms around her, and then I lifted her into my own arms. Some moments in life are just totally filled with God. That was one of them.

Two years later, we got another phone call. Another of our foster children had been turned back to the social services agency, and she was

Family life is where the two most powerful realities of existence, namely life and love, join together to create and add to the great harmonics of the universe.

in the psychiatric unit of Denver Children's Hospital. It did not take us three weeks to decide this time; it was more like three seconds.

So now we find ourselves once again attending parents' meetings at the local school, monitoring homework assignments, and occasionally seeing various children's movies at the local theater (and, quietly, apart from their always attentive ears, rating which ones are really the worst).

We are fortunate to have the supportive care and assistance of our older children. Our new experience of parenting is fully a family venture. We had consulted with our older children before we decided to adopt. After all, we were no longer considered young anymore. There were actuary tables to consider.

It is now a few years later, which means that my wife and I both qualify for most senior discounts. We continue to learn new things every day about the adventure of family living as we face the challenges of parenting at the same time we are experiencing the blessings of grandparenting. Family life for us remains the primary way we see God calling us to holiness. And on our good days, we get close to appreciating that. We often realize it is within family that people become who they are. Family life is where the two most powerful realities of existence, namely life and love, join together to create and add to the great harmonics of the universe. It is where all of us learn a basic meaning of life, where our hearts are first broken open to savor the entwined mystery of human love and divine love. Family expressions of love and acceptance breathe life into the crevasses and contours of what makes each of us human.

Family spirituality is somewhat hidden from view, sacramental in form, deeply communal, faithful to the spiritual traditions of the church, often hopeful, and always loving. It has a playful side to it. It has its moments of zesty celebration and honest prayer. Sometimes it is declared with song and dance. Sometimes with tears and silence. It is expressed in very worldly, rather messy ways, and it seasons both the life of the church and the rest of the world.

A key image that has helped me unwrap the spiritual riches of family life is the image of the heart. In many cultures the heart symbolizes the center of the person and is associated for obvious reasons with life. A pulsating heart is a sure indicator of vitality.

But there is more. In the Hebrew Scriptures, the poetic writers took up this image of the heart to speak of our relationship with God. A closed heart was considered deaf and unresponsive to God's transforming presence and word. It was as if the word of God entered the person, traveled to the heart, and bounced off its hardened surface. Without entrance into the heart, there was no possibility of divine influence. God's word could not take up residence in the person with a hardened heart.

On the other hand, an open heart, a heart that is softened by love, welcomes God's presence. It is like the morning light filling a darkened room. Thomas Keating, in writing about intimacy with God, describes how the light of faith, the enlightened heart, can pour into our lives, shedding light not only on us but also on absolutely everything and everyone around us.

Think of it: Raising children is an important part of the lives of a good segment of the population. But how often we miss the full, magnificent spiritual meaning of the commonplace. In reality, every authentic gesture of family care and concern is of spiritual importance.

I invite you to open your eyes and yourself to the presence of God within the ordinary, quotidian moments of family life. Raise your awareness that life is charged with the real presence and power of God's grace.

As I begin this reflection on the spiritual life of the family, I want to express gratitude to all the families who have given me life. My first family has changed some with the deaths of my mom and dad during the last decade. I firmly believe, however, that life still flows between us. My second family, the Congregation of Holy Cross, still plays a role in my life. Based on the vision of Father Patrick Peyton, founder of the Family Rosary, I remain connected with Holy Cross Family Ministries. They have provided me with moral and financial support to write this account. My present family is blessed with seven children and many grandchildren. (I will not give their number here because it seems to change rather regularly.) Family for me is a daily challenge, an abundant blessing, and the place—as Robert Frost once wrote—where they always have to take me in. I stand in wonder of its complexities and its constant place of importance in the great mystery of human life.

CHAPTER ONE

Heart-Charged Moments

Joys and sorrows,

hopes and disappointments,

births and birthday celebrations,

wedding anniversaries of the parents,

departures, separations and homecomings,

important and far-reaching decisions,

the death of those that are dear—

all these mark

God's loving intervention

into the family's history.

—John Paul II

"God's loving intervention." We have been taught, and truly want to believe, that God is involved in our family. But we often are like the blind in the Gospel: We don't see…until we finally do see.

For me, it happened one night early in our family life, during the washing of the kids' feet. Up until that moment, I was just doing my job, my fatherly part of our family's "going to bed" ritual. It was nothing really special—just a typical bathtime before bed for our two little ones, both under three. We lived in a rural area and our children loved the outdoors. Sometimes they brought some of the outdoors indoors. A quick wash before sleep was always appropriate.

During the three years I was pursuing my doctoral studies at the University of Notre Dame, we were living in a small house built by my wife's grandfather. It wasn't the Ritz, but it was perfectly adequate for us. It had all the essentials, but nothing beyond. Since we drew our water from a well beneath the house, we conserved water by bathing our little ones together. (Family economics can stretch pretty far if needed.)

The bathtub had been filled with water that was tinged slightly brown. We called it our "special mineral water." It gave our children's bodies a pleasing light brown cast—at least, that was our explanation to them. (We avoided mentioning to them that there was such a thing as clear water.)

I lowered each one into our special water. Once their bodies were partially submerged, I had to move quickly. Two sibs in confined quarters were always a dangerous mixture. I had the soap in one hand and a washcloth in the other. I worked from the older to the younger, from top to bottom, assembly-line style. Giggles and splashes filled the tiny bathroom.

The insight happened when I was near the end of my chore—the foot part, to be exact. I always paid extra attention to the crevasses between their tiny toes where all sorts of vermin might be lodged. As I cleaned the last of four little feet, I had a genuine family-style epiphany. An image of the Last Supper suddenly came to my mind. I saw Jesus taking a basin of water, kneeling down before his disciples, and washing their feet. Those apostolic feet were, no doubt, carrying some of the good earth from the day's travels, just as were the feet of my squirming little children.

I suddenly realized that I was following Jesus' way of doing things. In fact, I was doing exactly what he had done—washing the feet of those I loved. With an intensity that almost scared me, I felt God watching my actions—and smiling.

In that instant this mundane, ordinary, everyday sort of activity took on profound, even eternal meaning. I realized that I was privileged to be intimately involved in a sacred and holy act, the liturgy of the family. Just as God was acting through the person of Jesus, God was also present and active in me. Imagine that: God in our bathroom; God through me washing two pairs of tired, dirty feet; God playing the role of the Majestic Footwasher.

At that moment, I entered—or, more accurately, was pushed into—the wondrous world of family spirituality. It wasn't described with those words back then because the language of the spiritual life of the family wasn't in common use. If used at all, it mostly focused on religious devotions or involvement in church activities. It was not about baths, messy family meals, and responses in the middle of the night to a child's request for water. It was not about the inherently ordinary, but it should have been.

All caring family gestures are essentially spiritual and sacred. At any particular moment, they are among the most spiritual events happening across the face of our planet. The perspective I gained during that bathtub moment was truly a gift from God, a special grace that opened my heart and allowed me to experience that mysterious joining of heaven and earth. I have come to realize that everything that serves the life of our family is holy.

The opening of my eyes during that evening bath has gradually extended into a 24/7 application. I have found that spirituality can be at home with each distinct event that makes up the family's daily routine. It can be incorporated into the struggle to accompany everyone to a safe harbor at end of the day. It can illuminate our attempts to stay connected with each other. It can elevate every effort to care for, love and help each other.

I am reminded of Mother Teresa's dedication to the idea that God works though us, or as she once put it, we are "a pencil in the hand of God, writing a love letter to the world." She believed that every act done for another person in this world should be a specific act of deep love. No matter how small or insignificant the act, when done with love, it becomes great. How important for families to know this.

Unfortunately, love letters to the world and bathtub epiphanies are not the norm. For most of us, the days and nights of our lives roll on with fairly routine activities, blessed by a few highlights along the way. Lofty thoughts of God and love take a back seat to meals, laundry and bills. Life throws us a few curves once in a while, but we soldier on. The question is not whether we believe in God but how we can sense God's presence in the midst of the ordinary. Where does our spirituality intersect with our schedule? How do we combine our household with holiness? Where do we start?

A Sacred Perspective

The good news is that we can start right where we are, where our families are, in the nitty-gritty of daily life. No special courses needed. No advance degrees required. A shift in three core perspectives can make all the difference: wonder, awareness and watchfulness.

Be Open to Wonder

Any investigation—whether theological or educational or spiritual—works best when we begin with an attitude of wonder. And one of the best ways to develop an attitude of wonder is to see the world through our children's eyes.

Our youngest son and I were standing on the deck of our home one afternoon. A welcome summer rainstorm had just passed through, and we were enjoying the new freshness of the air, the glistening droplets still on the leaves of the tree next to us. And just like Noah of old, we were treated to a spectacular rainbow vividly spread across the sky. My son was five years old at the time, a good age for scientific investigation, because the whole world offers its wonders to new eyes not yet used to "the same old things." And being an educator myself, I thought this was one of those teachable moments. So I asked him, "Timmy, what do you think rainbows are made of?"

He was silent for quite a while as his brain tried to decipher this magnificent display of nature's creativity. He looked at the sky and then turned to me with a huge, knowing smile on his face. "I know what it is. It's colored raindrops!"

He was right, although I would have never "seen" that in a million years. How perceptive and blessed we are when we allow the eyes of wonder to enlighten us.

Wonder is an amazing spiritual gift. Wonder creates openness to the wider and deeper dimensions of reality. Wonder awakens our imaginations to move beyond the obvious. Wonder opens us to the possibility of seeing more than we had first thought was there. Wonder is the spark that can fire our minds into flaming thoughts that give us new energy and enthusiasm for living. Wonder allows questions to be formed in their fullness, raising not only questions of "what is it?" but also "how can that be?"

Wonder helps us look for ways God is present in creation. Wonder invites us to ask, "If we are creatures made in God's image, what does that suggest about God?" Wonder, ultimately, is our capacity to sense God in our midst.

Be Aware of God's Presence

When I was a young boy, we lived next to a vacant lot. On the other side of the lot was a grocery store where my mom used to send me for bread and milk and other essentials. I have vivid memories of walking through that vacant lot at night. For me, it was often a daunting experience. My imagination could easily create dangerous presences all around me. If I thought about God in these circumstances, I could also quite easily slip over into thinking about devils and other desperados seeking to devour me. When I later learned (from Rudolf Otto's concept of the holy as that which is "numinous") that the experience of God can be both fascinating and fearful, I knew exactly what the fearful part was.

To be aware of God, the Creator of the entire universe, is no small matter. Annie Dillard has written that when we enter the sanctuary of the church for worship, we should be issued crash helmets at the door and seat belts in the pews. It might very well be a rough ride.

Awareness of God is one of the most basic and important ingredients of a vital spiritual life, and many theologians and philosophers have pondered this over the centuries. It is helpful to look at the geography of this investigation and note some of its major topographical features.

First, God is always hidden just below the surface of creation. Look wherever you want—to the heavens above or the earth below—and you will not see God. In applying this idea to family experience, we don't number God as one of our family members; God is not there in that way. To paraphrase an insight of the theologian Karl Rahner, God is not an object alongside other objects. God's invisibility or concealment, however, does not in any way imply absence. God exists in another realm and in a way that is totally unlike any reality in creation. While no thing is able to contain or be identified as God, any moment of authentic love involves God being there. All earthly love dissolves the hard barrier between the cold surface of life and the hot fiery presence of God.

That brings us to the second idea: that God's hiddenness and God's presence are inseparable. Even though we can't see God, God is nevertheless very present to us, and that divine presence sustains all of creation. At first glance, this may sound like double-talk, but it is simply our best attempt to capture through imagination, thought and language how God is both transcendent (beyond) and immanent (within) all creation and to us. Some call this God's mysterious presence.

What I take from all this is that God's presence can be seen, heard and felt, but not in an obvious way. Though God's presence is somewhat concealed, I like to add that it is very close to the surface. Understanding this dynamic—that God is in human reality, just out of sight—is most helpful in finding God's presence in the often very mundane world of family life.

Be Present to One Another

What does all this mean for family spirituality? Bottom line: To experience God's presence, we have to look more intensely, listen more carefully, think more imaginatively and feel more attentively. We need to be more present to the moment of living, especially as it happens each day. We need to be alert.

None of God's creatures seems more easily distracted than we humans. Right now my family is hosting a group of rabbits that live on our property. (Let's call them uninvited guests.) One trait they share with all their animal friends is vigilance. If one of our children enters their territory, the rabbits immediately go on extreme alert. Otherwise, they are on "regular" alert. Always, they're watchful.

We humans, on the other hand, can easily depart from the cares and concerns of our immediate world and enter into a thousand other worlds of our own making. I know: I was a classroom teacher for thirty-five years. Like all teachers, I could write a book on student distractibility.

Over the years, one of the things that I have admired in reading Annie Dillard is her rare ability to be aware of what's happening around her, especially in the outdoor world of nature. She can spend pages describing the flight of a bird or the movement of a beetle across a log. It is as if she misses nothing; she seems so thoroughly present to the world of nature around her.

The great Jewish philosopher Martin Buber speaks of the need for "being present to each other" in his discussion of an I-Thou encounter. In the midst of the precious moment of an I-Thou encounter, our full aware-

It is as if the rest of the world has disappeared, and we are fully and completely there, just the two of us.

ness, our complete attention and focus, is riveted on the other. It is as if the rest of the world has disappeared, and we are fully and completely there, just the two of us.

I admire people who in the course of a conversation give me the feeling that I am the only one in the world for them at that moment. It is really an overwhelming feeling. That's one of the special gifts I have received from our adopted children. On occasion, they tell my wife and me how much they appreciate us and our decision to bring them into our family. This doesn't happen all the time. Family life doesn't work that way. We easily slip into routines, and it's okay to take each other for granted most of the time. But there are those special, very holy moments when these kids look at me and I look at them just not as objects with labels but as persons, sharing our lives in a deeply significant way. These moments may be fleeting, like a bird alighting on a tree branch and then flying away, but they are among life's most important and impressionable events. In the middle of them we experience God.

A Sacred Pathway

To be truly present—whether with our family or with God—we need to keep a sacred pathway open between us. Mostly, we need a greater openness to what and who is around us. We need open eyes and ears, along with an open heart.

To do that, we need to identify what might be standing in the way. We must honestly examine our attitudes and our current emotional state of mind to identify any blockages to the free flow. There is a Latin phrase from medieval theologians that I love: removens prohibens. It is almost poetic when you say it out loud. Literally, it means the removing of what's preventing us from openness to God's graced presence.

There are four factors, in particular, that can get in the way, keeping us blind and deaf to God's activity: anxiety, stress, clouded vision, and fear. Fortunately, our blindness and deafness can be healed.

Quiet the Noise

During the Eucharist liturgy, after the Lord's Prayer, there is a short prayer that includes a petition to lessen our anxiety. What may appear to be simply a prayer for better mental health is really a request to heal one of the greatest obstacles to living a deep human life, a rich family life, and an intense, enthusiastic spiritual life. I am speaking of the presence of harmful, even debilitating, anxiety.

One of the first requirements for creating a path to an awareness of God's abiding presence is to lessen the psychic noise of anxiety in our lives. Too much noise prevents us from hearing the quiet, sometimes whispering, voice of God.

I have been helped in my life as an educator, spouse and parent by the insights of the esteemed family therapist Edwin Friedman. He was a Jewish rabbi who focused most of his work on how to best effect healthy change in families and in religious communities—which operate in many ways like a large family. For both social entities, he said there was a singularly important personal trait needed by those who wanted to move in the direction of health and vitality. He called it "non-anxious presence." It was his conviction that we cannot really help others if our own problems are always screaming for attention. Friedman taught therapists and others who sought leadership roles in communal change to learn the discipline of non-anxious presence by identifying, in detail, what caused anxiety and fear in their own life.

Friedman also taught that for a family to change its destructive interpersonal dynamics someone in the family needs to step outside the anxiety field that dominates the family relationships to see what is needed for improvement. In other words, to see what is going on at deeper levels within our family we first need to be free of the ear-shattering noise. We have to become people of interior peace in order to initiate change for the better.

What a powerful idea! Being a non-anxious presence allows us to stand right in the midst of the storm and yet remain calm. I am reminded of how Jesus always remained at peace, even during the most trying of circumstances. On one occasion, a sudden storm on the Sea of Galilee caught his disciples off guard and created some very fearful moments for them. Jesus was with them—peacefully asleep in the bottom of the boat. The disciples shook him awake and pleaded with him to do something: They might capsize any minute; he needed to save them right now.

I like to imagine Jesus slowly opening his eyes and giving them a big smile. But not moving. They continue in their state of sheer panic while he calmly asks, "Is there a problem?" As they assail him with pleas and more panic, Jesus yawns and slowly stretches. Eventually he stands up, takes delight in the furies of nature smashing against the side of the boat, and calms the sea.

Or perhaps he simply allowed his non-anxious presence to spill over into them. Maybe they took on his spirit and rode the waves like a bunch of kids enjoying a first-century amusement park ride. My inclination is to conclude that the sea was not calmed, but rather the spirit of the disciples was made calm as they began to experience the storm in a new way.

Just as the disciples' fear and anxiety prevented them from receiving the abiding peace that Jesus had told them only God can give, I cannot imagine living a vital spiritual life in a family while being filled with anxiety. Anxiety can create psychic noise so powerful that it obliterates the sound of any other voice. God did not create us to be anxious but to be people who lived in the spirit of personal peacefulness.

Focus on Priorities

While the presence of serious anxiety is certainly one of the major obstacles to finding God's presence in our everyday family lives, destructive stress is its close cousin. Stress, which is simply the body's way of preparing itself for strenuous activity, arises as we meet the many ordinary challenges of life. In the caves that were the most common home of humanity for most of its history, the appearance of a saber-toothed tiger at the cave's opening was an occasion for stress. Under those circumstances, stress was good; it was necessary for survival.

Today, stress can arise when we suddenly meet a traffic snarl on the freeway or worry about the economy or think about the uncertain future of our children. Stress activates the body for a powerful reaction. Chemicals are produced and then shot throughout the body. Our bodies are amazing reaction systems, but too much stress, too much over-reaction to life, can

While the presence of serious anxiety is certainly one of the major obstacles to finding God's presence in our everyday family lives, destructive stress is its close cousin.

threaten us from within. Everything we have learned from research, for example, points to the connection between stress and heart attacks.

I have had a great teacher in this area, Father James Gill, a Jesuit psychiatrist, who was on the research team that originally surfaced the link between stress and heart failure. He taught that stress could be a killer if not addressed and defused. I also learned this lesson—the hard way, I may add—from my own cardiologist after I had to endure two angioplasties. His advice was simple and direct: "David, you need to relax more. We've had to open your heart arteries twice. Find ways to relieve stress or else…." I knew the rest of what he was going to say.

Chronic unaddressed stress is terribly harmful not just to our bodies but to our spirits as well. It can drain precious energy from our limited resources. It can suck the enthusiasm out of life. It can modify how we think about time. A stressful person tends to think about time as an enemy rather than a friend. In times of crisis, a stressed person tends to focus almost exclusively on the danger while ignoring everything else that is going on. Stressed-out people tend to focus only on their own survival. In a sense, stress is totally self-serving. While stress is sometimes good and necessary, chronic stress not only shortens the lives of thousands, it also depletes the lives of millions.

Just like anxiety, stress can limit our perceptive ability. Research shows that under stress, our eyesight tends to narrow as if a charging rhino is attacking us. We need to realize, too, that the body does not distinguish between real attack and humanly imagined attack.

One of the most important skills of the spiritual life is to determine what is really important and what is not. More and more this has to be done because our culture comes at us saying that everything is important. Most commercials have as a sub-theme that the product being sold is so important that we need it to be happy, fulfilled or even to survive.

Did you ever try to get a child to understand the difference between want and need? If you have been successful, write a book. A million parents will buy it. We can all be seduced into thinking not only that we can have it all but also that we need it all. Here's a small, but telling example. I must confess that there have been times when I didn't take one or another of our children shopping. I know the traps that are out there to snare the appetites of children. They don't put the candy at the grocery-store checkout just because they couldn't find a spot near the milk or soup cans. At that moment, having a candy bar can become the most important "need" in the child's life. Priority number one! And we adults can suffer a similar kind of pressure. Our whole society is built around moving new products into our lives and our already filled homes.

To counter this, a wonderfully needed social revolution is spreading across the land. It's called many things, but it's mantra is, "Simplify, simplify, simplify." It's about attending to what's really important and withdrawing from the rest. I see this as an important part of every family's spiritual life.

Look Deeper

Seeing has always played an important part in the spiritual life. To sense the presence of God in our life, we have to be able to see more than is readily apparent. We need to be able to see not only the beautiful rose before us but also the mind that created it in the first place. We have to be able to see through surfaces into a deeper realm.

When Jesus was about to teach his disciples an important truth, he would often begin by curing someone's blindness. (In fact, I wonder whether his curing blindness ranks in symbolic importance right behind his restoring life to the dead.) We might well say that Jesus came to dwell among us to teach us how to see. Good vision is an absolute essential for living the spiritual life. Seeing God always requires twenty/twenty spiritual eyesight. Paul said it as well as anyone: We see God only through a glass darkly.

If one is preoccupied with aphids that might infiltrate one's roses—or the homework that is still undone—then there is little likelihood of seeing even a glimpse of God in that moment. This is not to say that aphids and homework aren't important concerns. They are. But if that is all we think about, then that is all we will see.

In family life, we need to see in each child the love of God that first created this unique and beautiful human being. This can be especially challenging to parents today in an age when children can appear more as projects, financial burdens, or added responsibilities to an already crowded life. That's why "looking deeper" is so important. We all need reminders of the Big Picture, which includes a response to the deeper reasons why each of us exists at all and how we play important roles in each other's lives. God is deeply interested in each of us. We do well to live in accord with this powerful truth.

Be at Peace

I have found it interesting that the most common phrase in the New Testament is "Be not afraid." It occurs over two hundred times. It was also the most common phrase uttered by John Paul II. Given the frequency of this invitation, we can surely assume that we have some control over this matter.

Years ago, when I was teaching at Regis University, which was founded and is staffed by the Jesuits, I experienced the Spiritual Exercises of Ignatius Loyola. One of the greatest gifts I received from these marvelous meditations was the realization that God decidedly wants us to be at peace. Up until that time, I had thought that God wanted us to be trying very hard all the time to be saints. Such effort implied that we should constantly stand in the tension between the ideal God wanted and the reality of our ordinary lives.

Through a prayer period that is part of the Spiritual Exercises, I came to see this "battle" as a sure-fire formula for producing great stress. Call it an unmitigated demand for perfection. Call it workaholism with a spiritual veneer. Through reflection and prayer, I came to understand that we can become harder on ourselves than God intends.

In my family of origin, I am a firstborn son. So was my father. That multiplies the impact. Those who study family birth order point out that firstborns receive more attention and more pressure to succeed than other siblings born into the same family. They tend to be super responsible, over-achievers, and often very hard on themselves. They cannot rest until the job is done. They cannot play until all the items of their lengthy "to do" list are crossed off.

I can easily identify with those deep pressures. They are the background noise, the inner voice that reminds me oftentimes of my many unfinished life projects. I have benefited greatly from the writings of Richard Carlson, who basically started a cottage industry around that old piece of wisdom, "Don't sweat the small stuff." I know now that we can best accomplish this task while dwelling in the peace given to us by God through Christ. The tranquil spirit more easily detects God's presence.

Family life offers a million distractions, as it should. Unless unusually gifted, we who are given the responsibility of caring for children float in and out of the awareness of God's presence on the best of days. Sometimes we forget about God entirely because a child is sick or a spouse is worn down by money fears or job worries. We can create crooked roads with lots of twists and turns. We can make connecting with God much more difficult than it need be. God is always coming our way, because God is already in our midst.

* * *

If you haven't gotten the point yet, I will say it as clearly as I can: Our life with God and our family life are one. The life of ordinary families is filled with God. The spirituality of family life is living as family.

That's what I learned while washing those squirming little feet many years ago. With what I can only call God's wake-up grace, I connected my act of service with something larger and quite real: God's loving presence in the midst of ordinary family life.

Ordinary Families

It's not by a financial statement
or by highlighted trophies or prizes
that families gain wealth.
Lasting family fortune is amassed
by creating and depositing
a million human heart-charged moments
into the heart of God.

In families everywhere
flashes of brilliance burst forth
from loving glances at morning light,
from hugs served with orange juice and real maple-syruped pancakes,
in the flutter of quick airborne kisses at the door on the way out,
from cell phone midday checks to learn if all is well,
and from nighttime visits to a child or a grandma,
bedded down beneath a soft blanket.

Witness this alchemic reaction
as fierce human particles of love
forge gold through fiery embraces
of bodies blessed and broken,
their lives rubbing together
melting disparity and smoothing hard edges.
This furnace warms cold hearts and defrosts icy words.

Families burn to life like coalesced heated galaxies
formed by the gravity of mattered persons drawn together
in dance, song and sweat
while all the time swirling around
an intense loving center
that is the deepest mystery of all.

CHAPTER TWO

Ordinary Holiness

The family finds in the plan of God,
the creator and redeemer,
not only its own identity, what it is,
but also its mission, what it can and should do.
The role that God calls the family to perform in history
derives from what the family is;
its role represents the dynamic
and existential development of what it is.
Each family finds within itself a summons
that cannot be ignored and
that specifies both its dignity and responsibility.

—John Paul II

Like many families, ours takes an awful lot of pictures of ourselves. In fact, our family has boxes and boxes of them. If we were more organized, we would have them in albums, each labeled with the time and place of the particular pictures. But we don't. I sometimes envy those families who are more organized than ours, but then I come to my senses and simply note that each family is different. And I remind myself that our disorganization leads to many surprises.

One of my favorite family photos was taken when our four children welcomed child number five into their midst. Our four older children are sitting rather close together on our living room sofa so they can all fit into the picture. Our daughter, the eldest, is holding the blanketed bundle of new life in her arms. On the face of each child is a look of happiness, along with what seems to be a kind of question mark.

They were all still quite young, but somehow they intuitively knew that some things were about to change. They realized that the new arrival was a wondrous gift to our family, but they also felt impending loss. With the coming of the new arrival, they were losing some of mom and dad's time, some space in the home. And there was one more mouth to consume the family's finite supply of ice cream. There would be gains, but there would also be losses.

Whenever I look at this picture today, I see God's creative love at work. I also felt it when I took the picture almost thirty years ago. That event on the sofa, that moment when our children welcomed their new brother into our family, was a family sacramental moment.

Simply stated, sacramentality means that God is present everywhere and within everything in creation. The Catholic Church has focused a major part of its life around seven sacraments, seven special rituals, where God is present and active. Most Christian churches have similar rituals. I see a rich connection between these formal sacraments of the church and the informal sacraments of the home.

The sacramental moments of family life share the same spirit, the same grace, and the same divine presence, but they are enacted *in a family way.* Holiness in the family takes on a very ordinary appearance.

Family sacraments can be disorganized, spontaneous or messy, and they often don't appear very religious at all. But done with a generous spirit, these seemingly worldly activities are the raw material out of which great sanctity is carved. Much like the ordinary appearance of Jesus to his contemporaries, these moments often hide a sacred richness, a spiritual treasure beyond measure.

Family sacraments are part of what John Paul II called *the church of the home* or *the domestic church.* These domestic events are not alternatives to the formal sacraments of the church but rather occasions of God's bestowal of grace, moments when God enriches the life of the family and its members with holy vitality and celebration. They happen in the home because God's presence, love and power are there without limit. They materialize at home because God deeply desires to be part of our family life. God is there whenever we open our hearts to the flow of divine love.

There are three sacraments in the Catholic Church that are grouped together as the "sacraments of initiation": Baptism, Confirmation and Eucharist. Together, they form a foundational pattern, attending to the beginning of the Christian life, its early development, and its celebration in gratitude.

Family sacraments exhibit a similar basic Christian understanding that life includes experiences of suffering, sacrifice and death—all overcome by genuine altruistic love. This fundamental passage from death to life is played out in a thousand ways in family life. How often do we as parents set aside personal plans because a sick or lonely child needs our attention? How often do we give our energy and time to a spouse when needed? How hard do we work to bring bread to the table?

Sacramentality demands a gift of vision: We can see God's presence only with the eyes of faith.

Sacramentality is a rich, time-tested concept, but it can also be elusive because it lacks concreteness. By its very nature, the sacramentality of anything is not apparent. Only some kind of revelation, an awareness that penetrates to a deeper realm, brings it to the surface. Sacramentality demands a gift of vision: We can see God's presence only with the eyes of faith.

Seeing with deeper eyes is a major part of family spirituality, and God invites us—even desires us—to become aware of the divine dimension of ordinary life, of God's loving presence in the community of family.

A Celebration of Life

Does not our faith alert us to the powerful presence of God, especially at times when new life comes into being and death gives birth to eternal life? Birth and death are the two bookends that hold life here on earth together, and each shift in reality is the occasion for sacred rituals. Think of all the activities that accompany both births and deaths—everything from baby showers to Irish wakes. These are not radical ideas but thoughts that come from the center of our faith. They are at the heart of the Sacrament of Baptism and form a distinct starting point for family spirituality. In reality, every time the new replaces the old, family spirituality is filled with baptismal moments.

If asked when they have felt close to God, many people mention events directly connected with birth in the family. Certainly my wife has told me that she was keenly aware of God's presence when our children were born. Perhaps the most profound of all sacramental experiences for me was when our two adopted children were baptized. While I have intentionally not said much about their adoption, I will say that their journey to us was extremely perilous and difficult. Our decisions to adopt them were among the most difficult my wife and I ever made. So their baptisms filled me with a deep sense of blessing and responsibility.

Experiences around death in the family form the other side of journey, however. Religious scholars have noted that all religions are in some way a response to death. We seek ways to understand that somehow life continues both for the person who has died and for those who loved him or her. Family spirituality comes to the surface during those difficult times.

For example, I was blessed by having both my parents live into their nineties, but their departure from our earthly family life was accompanied still by deeply sad moments for my sisters and myself. The rituals we experienced at my mom's death carried that deep connection between death and life. At her wake, our family recited the family rosary, a custom that went back to when we were small children. My brother-in-law read a Jewish prayer affirming life, just before the casket was closed.

Then my immediate family—my dad, my sisters and I—were ushered into a limo that was supplied by the funeral home. But before the procession left for the short drive to the church, one of my sisters made an unexpected request: "Did anyone get mom's rosary?" she asked. We all looked at each other, a little baffled, and said that we hadn't. "But I want *that* rosary," she quickly responded. (As an historical footnote, I had actually made that rosary when I was in the seminary forty years before.)

My sister jumped out of the limo and stormed into the funeral parlor. Two minutes later, she victoriously rejoined us, tightly clutching the rosary, saying, "They had to reopen it, but I've got it."

But the scene was not over. One of my other sisters chimed in: "You know, I really like that dress mom was wearing. And I think it's my size too!" We all laughed heartily. There was still a lot of life in this family, even in the midst of what was one of our saddest family times together.

Such stories can be experienced as rich sacramental events. Life sometimes includes loss and attendant grief, for something has to give way to make room for the new: A new job or career is preceded by the loss of a job; a new place of residence suggests the loss of another home with all its familiarity; a return to good health means that one was once ailing; a return to healthy relationships within the family implies there had been a falling out.

A realistic family spirituality can be built on the hope-filled view that God is always on the side of life. The miracle of new life can come forth at any time. What we need is sensitivity to its miraculous happening. This is part of the "culture of life," an idea so vigorously preached by John Paul II.

When our first adopted daughter returned to our family at the age of three, after her previous adoptive family had decided not to keep her, she came back to us filled with confusion, fear and apprehension. Every evening she requested a bath, but not your ordinary "dip and dry" variety. She wanted a very *long* bath. She considered an hour in the tub the minimum. She also required that either my wife or I sit by the tub and talk with her while she soaked.

Clearly, her evening bath meant more than just washing the day's dirt from her little body. It was her way of returning to us through the waters. Moses would understand exactly what was going on with her at the deeper level. So would John the Baptist and Jesus. And with eyes of faith, so can we.

There is a Jewish prayer that celebrates each new morning as if it were a miracle: Out of the darkness of night, there arises new light. A cynical view of this would say, "Well, what did you expect? That the sun wouldn't rise?" But such a response misses the point. Believing in God's support of the life of the entire universe, a support that if taken away would plunge the universe into the darkness or nothingness from which it came, brings the believer to celebrate and give thanks for each and every sunrise. So let us live in the ongoing miracle of new life that comes in a thousand ways.

Rites of Passage

Look at the lilies of the field; see how they grow. Look at humans; see how we grow. Look at families; see how they grow. Life is a continual journey, a pilgrimage to our eternal home with God. It progresses over the many hills and valleys of life, and we experience a sequence of events that bring growth, maturation, progress and movement.

When I received the Sacrament of Confirmation as a young man in the 1950s (a time when a very muscular Catholicism was advanced as the ideal), I received images of defending the faith and standing up to the powers of evil in the world. I knew this would demand courage and valor. The ritual included a slap on the cheek by the bishop. I walked away after receiving Confirmation believing that I was stronger and more able to resist whatever challenged my faith.

Confirmation recognizes that a child is taking a big step into the world, and there are many parallels in the typical experiences of families, especially during those transition years from childhood through adolescence into young adulthood. Family life is filled with rites of passage that are confirming, transition moments.

When recently presenting this idea to a gathering of religious education professionals, I asked what would be an example of this kind of event in the family. Immediately a voice shouted from the back of the room: "Driver's license. It changes everything. It means one has wheels to the great outside world."

This suggestion stimulated a spirited discussion because it was so much on target. The acquisition of a driver's license is a major rite of passage in our culture. One's status is changed, along with the acquiring of a whole new set of responsibilities. For the family, it means an extra driver to get bread and milk from the local store. Perhaps Mom's role as soccer chauffeur can now be shared with the new driver.

But how many families see and experience this major moment in a teen's life as part of their spiritual life? Even though a major alteration in family dynamics takes place, there is usually no thought or word about God to highlight the moment. But there could be. Unfortunately, there are no church blessings or rituals for a driver's license (although some innovative pastors bless cars and encourage devotion to St. Christopher). Perhaps the family can create a meaningful ritual on its own. Bless the teen and bless the license. Talk about new opportunities and responsibilities. The child is growing up. Something is passing away and something is beginning. This is God's plan for life: that we progress as persons. Transition milestones call for celebration!

What about other growth events in the family? Celebrations such as birthdays and anniversaries can be more than occasions for gift giving when we bring God into the picture. Some families light a child's baptismal candle on each birthday. Some married couples express a renewal of their commitment before each other and before God on their anniversary. Certainly various graduations qualify as family confirmational events. God has assisted in giving the strength, the energy and the ability to reach each new plateau of accomplishment. God gives the life and supplies the growth. And with courage and enthusiasm, families can respond in joy-filled gratitude.

The Sacred Meal

It is really amazing to me how many times the Gospels mention the involvement of Jesus with eating. He seemed to go from one meal to another. In fact, Luke's Gospel is basically built around ten meals. (I once wondered whether our common image of Jesus as relatively thin was inaccurate. Then I was reminded that he walked from meal to meal, which helped him stay lean.)

Seriously, I think God became human in part to experience eating with us. God was hungry for our love, just as we thirst for God's love. And Jesus eventually offered himself as food for our journey through life. You can't get much more basic than that.

Food and feasting are symbolic cornerstones of faith. One of the biblical symbols for God's entrance into our world was Jesus turning water into wine at the wedding feast. Jesus also made it a point to eat with the marginalized in his society, as a symbolic gesture of divine inclusion. And you can be sure that Jesus' adversaries always noticed (disapprovingly) who ate with him. They made certain that everyone knew that Jesus ate with despised tax collectors and public sinners, such as prostitutes. When they protested that Jesus could not be from God because he allowed sinners at his table, he responded by saying that he did this to show that everyone was offered new life from God. Jesus ate with people not just to remedy human hunger, but also to satisfy their hunger for God.

When the first Christians gathered, often under dangerous circumstances, they celebrated God's abiding love with a love feast, or *Agape*. These prayerful gatherings brought them together to remember what Jesus had done and to share the community's gifts with each other, especially with the less fortunate. These gatherings brought everyone into a relationship of equality, and the distinctions that often pulled people apart—gender, background and social status—were judged meaningless for this kind of feast. This initial sense of communal oneness was eroded by human narrowness and selfishness, and the radical nature of the *Agape* became somewhat blurred. However, it remains, even today, as an ideal and as an expression of our basic oneness before God.

No prayer of Jesus was more heartfelt than when he prayed that we all may be one, as he was one with God. According to John's Gospel, it was during the Last Supper that he prayed this stirring prayer before he took bread, blessed it, broke it and then shared it. These are all symbolic actions of deep spiritual importance for our families today.

Blessing the bread is a recognition that this food is from God; it is sacred in origin. Of course, it comes through the work of humans—those who grow the grain, harvest it, grind the wheat into flour, mix flour with other ingredients, bake the bread, and bring it to the hands of the one reciting the blessing. Yet, ultimately, bread comes from God. Think about God's initial creation of the universe. God both created and assembled the ingredients that would eventually become bread and wine and asparagus and apples. Talk about foresight and planning! So we bless bread, for starters, while realizing that in the big picture of creation, all food is sacred.

Then the bread is broken. The symbolism of breaking bread is as old as human memory. A loaf of bread is not to be sustenance for one, but for many. It is broken so that it can be shared and made available for communal nourishment. Brokenness is a sign of vulnerability and availability.

The image of being broken open for others is the essence of the life of Jesus: Through his brokenness, we are shown God's openness.

The bread is then shared with all those who are present. Often the Gospel accounts of feeding report that Jesus' disciples distributed the bread to the multitudes. Many see this as a symbolic indication that we are to nourish the spiritual lives of all who come to enjoy the great festival of God's generous love. Everything given is to be shared.

This symbolism of sharing a meal has an inherent connection with the common family meal, where food and conversation are shared. If you're thinking, "What's so sacred about the family eating together?" I'll be quick to say that it is not obvious because too many families dismiss the family meal. For too many, the act of eating has been reduced to a functional, mundane necessity of refueling.

But when we consider a meal's basic symbolic elements, we begin to see the spiritual parallels. First, it is worth remembering how the food arrived at the family table. Where did its journey begin? Whose effort was needed to transform meats, fruits, vegetables and grains into what we are eating? When we understand how much it took to make it possible for us to eat, our awareness of the meaning and value of food increases, as well as our gratitude and respect for our brothers and sisters who labor in the fields. As children are taught this, and adults remember it, it becomes part of the family spirituality.

Then there is the simple act of eating together, sharing the same food around the table. It is spiritually important to be conscious of each other's

Whatever time of day it is, the family meal can be an opportunity for family reconciliation and celebration.

presence. When the whole family is gathered to eat together, this is no small matter. It expresses our connection to each other and the value we place on one another.

Perhaps the most common complaint about contemporary families is that the parents and children are not together enough on an average day. Everyone is going about his or her agenda. Each one follows an individual schedule. If paths cross, it's often just for a passing "hello." For this reason, I am a strong advocate of families eating together. It doesn't have to be every meal. Maybe breakfast is better than an evening meal. Maybe eating out together is a viable option. Whatever time of day it is, it can be an opportunity for family reconciliation and celebration. In fact, I would go so far as to say that I consider the family meal as the family's form of a Eucharistic meal.

I once shared this idea in a talk that I was giving, and someone in attendance responded rather angrily, "Do you mean that you are reducing the mass to being nothing more than a common family meal?" My first thought was that perhaps I really was overstating my point because I felt so strongly about it. But I held to my conviction and answered, "No, I am not trying to reduce the mass to an ordinary family meal. I am trying to raise the meaning of an ordinary family to something like the mass."

The family meal is a special family way of celebrating the presence of God in our midst. It is an opportunity for prayer and play. It is a place where family life can reach a certain crescendo of intensity.

In our family, we have a custom at our evening meals together that we call "plusses and minuses." It goes like this. Once everyone has filled his or her plate with food, one family member leads grace and initiates the ritual of sharing the day. (When our family numbered seven, each of us led one day of the week.) Then, like the passing of food, the telling of the day's events for each person begins. We have a rule that each person has to disclose at least one positive and one negative aspect of the day. (I suppose part of our shared family belief is that no day is perfect. There are always minuses.) Another rule is that everyone has to participate. Free-flowing conversation does not begin until each family member has had his or her moment.

As a parent, I have found this ritual a remarkably painless (and somewhat deceptive) way of finding out what is going on in the lives of our children, especially as they were passing through their turbulent teen-age years. We started this custom when our children were small, and almost thirty years later we are still doing it.

Research in family life has clearly shown that the family exercises the most powerful influence of all social institutions in the formation of beliefs and values in children. The family is a "school of love," as John Paul II so appropriately called it. What we learn in family will last a lifetime—for better or worse. And I believe that much of that connection, education and formation can happen around the ordinary family table.

I offer one final family example, again from my own experience. Recently, I was surprised just before midnight when one of our adopted daughters suddenly appeared in our kitchen as I was locking up the house for the night. She had gone to bed a few hours earlier, and my initial reaction was to get her back to bed.

"Dad, I can't get to sleep," she said as she looked at me, obviously thinking that I had some magic formula to help her. She continued. "Dad, you know that tea you sometimes take to help you sleep? Can I have some?"

(I sometimes take a cup of herbal tea that is supposed to bring on sleep more easily. It seems to work, but I never quite know whether it is really the tea or just the slowing down to relax and enjoy it.)

So at the bewitching hour of midnight, my daughter and I prepared two cups of tea and had our little meal. It became for me, and I hope for her, an almost mystical moment. Fortunately, I was able to truly hear what she wanted, which was my presence. It wasn't a full family feast, but I would have to say that while we drank tea together at our family table I felt my heart burning within me. I suspect she felt some of the same.

This process of learning to love in the family is a most significant way to experience the Paschal Mystery, the passage from sin to grace. It is not a mystical concept reserved for scholars and theologians but a process that takes place within the dynamics of basic human life.

I am reminded of the way Jesus spoke to people. Instead of using abstract or esoteric language, he talked about birds and sheep, wheat and grapes, water and lilies of the field. But he didn't speak about these things as a biologist or chemist. He was a rabbi, a teacher, who taught his listeners how to see underneath the surface of things. He knew there was a formidable connection between creation as a work of divine art and the Artist from whose mind and heart all creation came into being. He showed that God could be found in and through human experience, in and through the world of creation.

Just as God's life was rendered into Jesus' human life as food shared at table and on hillsides, so too can families know the divine presence in ordinary places. God's Spirit leads us along the way. In family life, this way passes by bathtubs and the dinner table.

The Wonder of Water

Who made all this water?
wonders the little girl
gazing to where sea and sky meet.
Her little toes press into the moist sand
at exactly the place
where the ocean's foaming fingers
touch the dry sand.

How long did it take
to collect all this water?
wonders her inquisitive mind,
and will it ever go away
and how deep is it in the middle
and how do boats float?
Her mind jumps from one question to another.

This wondrous water
beckons the child's mind
as her small cupped hands
try to hold it fast
but can't because the water always
slithers downward through tiny spaces
between little fingers.

Years later
the child will learn how life needs water to survive
and how oxygen and hydrogen unite.
But now, in days of innocence and wonder,
suddenly another water issue surfaces.
Instead of being held by heavier thoughts,
the child slowly walks
toward her fully-relaxed, sun-bathing, almost asleep mom,
carrying a red plastic bucket
once filled with sand but now to the very top
with chilled sea water.
Intent and focused,
moving resolutely
to re-baptize
guess who.

CHAPTER THREE

Ups and Downs

In and through
the events, problems, difficulties and circumstances
of everyday life,
God comes to the family,
revealing and presenting the concrete "demands"
of their sharing in the love of Christ for the church,
in the particular familial, social and ecclesial situation
in which they find themselves.

—John Paul II

In the decade after World War II, American families were presented with a very romanticized image of the family. Newly-minted television sets portrayed "perfect" families who were clean-cut, organized, well-behaved, and always able to solve their problems within a thirty-minute timeframe. Dads wore ties to the dinner table, and moms always wore dresses. The message of these imaginary portrayals of ordinary family life worked their way into our national imagination, and we thought of these TV families as ideals we should try to replicate.

Yet all families are blessedly human and imperfect. These two descriptors go hand in hand. Family life is life as it is lived in small, nourishing, life-giving groups. And it bears all the essential characteristics of being human—which means that it is never perfect. To over-idealize the notion of family is unrealistic, harmful, even potentially dangerous. To affirm family imperfection gives us a more realistic foundation for the spiritual life of our family.

I recall a conversation I had with one of my students who grew up in a family where alcohol abuse dominated the family's life. She had promised herself that when she had her own family there would be none of that. She eventually married and had kids, but she often found herself sad and disappointed. It wasn't until she had sought the help of a wise therapist that she uncovered her "problem." It seems that in ridding herself of the alcoholic family she didn't want, she had replaced it with an unrealistic image of family life, drawn largely from movies and television. When she tried to fashion her family in this ideal image, she was inevitably frustrated. Eventually, she was able to form a helpful view of family that corresponded to her actual wonderful family, with all its oddities and distinctive traits.

During the decades following World War II, family life faced many social pressures—from the cultural wars of the 1960s and 1970s and from the disease of "affluenza" that spread across the country in the 1980s and 1990s (which many say is still with us). Traditional or conventional values were under attack, and many became concerned that families were "falling apart."

It was during this time that the phrase "dysfunctional family" worked its way into everyday usage. First coined by psychologists, this description of family life was immediately adopted by journalists and the media as a shorthand way of describing the sorry state of contemporary families.

The idea of dysfunctionality comes from the world of mechanics, where each machine has to be in perfect working order in order to function well. A good operation depends on the job being done efficiently, quickly and without waste or error. When those who studied and described the world of interpersonal life and social groups, such as the family, adopted this language of mechanics, it implied that the "perfect" family functioned without difficulties, problems, confusion, misunderstandings, disagreements, or anything that would compromise them looking and operating well.

But, really, are there any perfect families that function perfectly all the time? The answer is no, at least not on this planet. I once asked a group of students who of them grew up in dysfunctional families. Every hand in the room was raised! It appears that we *all* need to be fixed.

Get Real

Why is it so important to mention the imperfect nature of all families? First of all, so that when we talk about family spirituality we're not led to think of idealized families. Families contain great amounts of disorder, frazzled nerves, and wholesale confusion. Families all experience ups and downs. God came to be with us precisely because we are imperfect human beings. It could be added that we also live in imperfect—albeit blessed and loved—families.

Our familial imperfections cover a wide spectrum. At one end are those matters that simply come with our common humanity: Our knowledge is always faulty; our awareness of others naturally ebbs and flows; our energy is limited. At the other end of the spectrum is moral fault: Not one of us can claim sinlessness; at times we all fall into acts of selfish greed; we all bend the truth to suit our own self-centered needs.

There is a distinction between sins of commission and sins of omission. Sins of *commission* are deliberate acts of hurting others, depriving them of what is theirs by right. We degrade another's good name, for example, or we take money that is needed for family survival and spend it on our own narrow interests.

Sins of *omission* are almost too many to list. These are the actions we *should* do if we truly love and respect each other, yet we fail to do them.

The root of most sins of omission is deep-seated selfishness. We *should* notice, but we don't. We *should* help with the dishes, but we're too tired. We *should* try to help another family member who is having a hard day, but we watch television instead. We *should* express our love and gratitude to each other, but we are silent.

Family spirituality calls us to address family imperfection. Doing this well is one of the most difficult parts of family spirituality. The task is ongoing: attempting to be truly good and loving of one another every day, with no time off, no vacations. Inevitably, there will be setbacks, difficulties and failures. How we deal with these brings us to the next important arena of family spirituality: the need for family forgiveness.

Healing Begins at Home

When Saint Thomas Aquinas discussed God's forgiveness, he noted that it happened in two settings. One is the *Sacrament of Reconciliation*, which is often simply called by Catholics "going to confession." The other happens in the ordinary course of interpersonal life. It may happen across the dinner table, in the car on the way to school, or in bed. The family has its own way of celebrating the great mystery of God's forgiveness. It can happen at any time.

Family Forgiveness

Many people say that the story of the Prodigal Son is one of their favorite Gospel stories. In part, I think this is because it is a story of family reconciliation. It is a story that we have all witnessed in some form or another. It is a story about us.

So many contemporary novels and movies use the restoration of family relationships as their primary theme. It is in our books and on our screens because it is a primary concern of our times. We know that families are no longer glued together by spiritual or societal glue—if they *ever* were. They operate more like free-spirited dancers who can dance together or alone.

Family separation can happen in all the interpersonal linkages within families. Marriage partners separate in all kinds of ways. Some end up by divorcing. Many older children distance themselves from parents. Sometimes the parent does the distancing. My own family has had many experiences of family separation because we have cared for so many foster children.

It's almost as if our present age were characterized by a reverse gravitational pull. Instead of growing closer together, families seem to be moving further apart. One societal indicator of this is the increasing number of people who live alone. There have always been members of society who chose the single life for a variety of reasons, but today we have singles in abundance. Recent demographic research points out that about half the adult households in the United States are headed by an unmarried person.

Family separation does not necessarily mean a physical leaving. Today's homes have more room in them than did the caves of our distant

Those from whom we derive some of the deepest experiences of love can also generate experiences of anger.

ancestors, and individuals can dwell in their own space and function quite well without much contact with others under the same roof. Then there is the distance of interpersonal tension. It can be triggered by something as small as a simple look of indifference. Living together causes difficulties and strain, and it takes very little to upend family harmony.

David Mace, a pioneer in the marriage enrichment movement, used to say that love and anger were two sides of the same coin. Because of our love for each other in marriage and in family life, we carry into our relationships many expectations of one another. Mace noted that, because it is not humanly possible to fulfill all the hopes and expectations we place on one another, disappointment is always around the corner.

And, as a spiritual aside, we cannot totally fulfill each other. We are created with an infinite desire for love. Part of the spiritual life is an acceptance that only God can satisfy that profound deep longing and hunger that comes from being created by God and for God.

Frustration is the immediate and automatic result of unmet expectation or needs, and frustration often generates anger. That means loving each other can cause us to be angry with each other. This is one of life's greatest paradoxes: that those from whom we derive some of the deepest experiences of love can also generate experiences of anger.

When I first learned of this dynamic, I was a bit skeptical. Now, after quite a few years of being married and a parent, I think David Mace's analysis is right on. He concluded that anger in itself does not result in interpersonal breakdown. It's what we do with the anger once we recognize it that spells the difference between renewed and severed relationships.

This area of our family life is directly linked with the Sacrament of Reconciliation. In both the formal, traditional sense and within the dynamics of family spirituality, reconciliation can be a great source of interpersonal growth and a wellspring for spiritual enrichment. It is another of those "from death to life" events. While the passage of time cures some of the hurt, usually it takes more. Reconciliation requires that someone express sorrow and regret and then ask for forgiveness. And there must be a return to another's heart. That's what the word *reconciliation* means: That which was once separated is now reconnected. It's a two-way street. Expression of sorrow meets acceptance of sorrow. Forgiveness is asked for and forgiveness is given. When this happens in the deeper parts of us, the part usually referred to as our heart, we sense an opening within us and a healing of what was broken between us. Genuine reconciliation is important for all of us, but especially for families.

A few years ago I gave a family retreat on the theme of family forgiveness. At one point, we talked about how a family knows when reconciliation has taken place. One person said that it was when silence turns into spirited conversation. Another said it was when someone finally goes to the refrigerator, opens the door, and the whole family enjoys a bowl of ice cream. One of the more interesting responses was from a person who said it was when their dad clears his throat. Sometimes family subtlety almost defies imagination. Everyone in that family knows this signal means, "It's all clear. We're back together again." But no outsider would recognize this important gesture of reconciliation.

Each family is unique, and each family will have some sacramental gestures that are all its own. I once heard this wise principle for marital survival: It take twenty acts of kindness to balance the hurt caused by a single hostile or critical word. I have often thought the figure "twenty" was a bit conservative.

One of the reasons why family reconciliation is so difficult is because a million threads connect family members to each other. Family disharmony hurts so deeply because these connections are intense. In fact, family criticism cuts deeper than criticism from outsiders *because* they come from family. Family events of hurt are not easily forgotten.

I once watched a telephone repairman attempt to reconnect a mass of neighborhood phone lines after a car had plowed into the box that housed the connections. There must have been more than a hundred different wires to reconnect before service could be restored. Family reconciliation is like that. Full communication is not easily restored if the communication wires have become severed.

Sometimes our actions bespeak reunion or reconciliation more than our words. Last year my wife and I decided to move from Colorado to Montana. (We have grown children in both places.) We could tell that our daughter who lived but a few miles from us south of Denver was deeply saddened by our move. Anger dwelt just beneath the surface. Our relationship seemed to deteriorate. Fewer words flowed between us, and visits were shorter and seemed terribly formal. Clearly, our connection with

That's the essence
of family reconciliation:
hearts reconnected
and love once again flowing.
It's one of the great miracles of life.

her and her family was strained. But just a few days before our moving date it was as if the ice between us had suddenly thawed: There she was, our daughter, working beside her mom, filling boxes and cleaning empty cabinets. She even declared her enthusiasm for the new experiences that would unfold for us almost a thousand miles to the north. That's the essence of family reconciliation: hearts reconnected and love once again flowing. It's one of the great miracles of life and clearly plays a major role in family spirituality.

Self-Forgiveness

I have one additional thought on family forgiveness that is directed more to parents than children. I suspect that not a few of us are afflicted with various ideas about family perfection. We want to carry in our purses and wallets pictures of perfect children. We want to be able to report in our Christmas letters the great accomplishments of our stellar children.

It would be better if we could ban any connection between the notion of the perfect family and our actual experience of family life. There are *no* perfect families. We may try to do everything right. We may try to be caring and considerate, but we all often fail.

So my recommendation to parents is that we could use a dose of self-forgiveness. We are created wonderfully human, which means that we are on a journey. We have not yet arrived. "Are we there yet?" a child on a journey asks incessantly. Our answer to ourselves when we ask the same question should be, "Not yet."

As parents, we experience limitations and shortcomings every day. Affirming and accepting this is not only a doorway to reality but also, I think, an important part of family spirituality. When we invite each family member to be more realistic about what's truly possible and to respect our imperfections, we can move on—not to become perfect but to become better. Then we can have a party—like the forgiving father threw for his Prodigal Son.

Healing Moments Not Covered by Health Insurance

The average family with small children consumes over ten thousand bandages in the course of raising one child. Probably only about one-third of those are really necessary; all the rest are given at the child's request for other reasons. And, while not medically required, a kiss is often given along with the bandage.

Years ago, my wife and I attended mass with her mother who was living with us. When the time came for processing forward to receive the Sacrament of Anointing, it was announced that anyone needing the healing power of the Lord should come forward. Immediately, my mother-in-law jumped up and headed forward. When she returned, I asked if she were sick. "No," she replied, "I'm just old, and that's enough! Some day you'll see."

Both of these examples touch on the reality that we are all in need of a healing touch; we are all on the edge of the line that separates health from sickness. Like the theological principle that we are all sinners, much the same can be said about sickness: We all suffer from one illness or another.

Taking care of family members during illness or hurt is a basic spiritual task of the family. And whenever we do this—with bandages and kisses or with hospital visits and flowers—we have the chance for a sacramental moment.

One of the missing pieces in today's medical culture is the family touch during times of illness. Too often healing is taken over by healthcare professionals. To be without family presence in a hospital or nursing home can be almost as painful as the condition that put one there in the first place.

Healing is a complex process, and it is connected with all aspects of human life. Loving human relationships are no small part of it. I believe God has gifted the family a portion of the healing ointment we all need. In fact, recent research into healing serious ailments such as cancer and heart disease have shown that someone's survival is greatly enhanced by the social support he or she enjoys, especially from family members. The mother or dad who brings a glass of cool water to a child with a high fever is as much a part of the healing process as the medicine a doctor brings.

Caring for the sick and infirm is often very difficult work. In family life this can be even more difficult because we are witnessing firsthand the suffering of someone we love deeply. But offering family care can also be an opportunity for profound spiritual enrichment. Where there is human suffering, God is close at hand. Where family is gathered in support of the afflicted one, there too is God.

Turning Family Chaos into Order

Most people I talk with "get" the close sacramental connections between what happens in the parish church and the church of the home—until we get to the Sacrament of Holy Orders. After all, ordination seems primarily for administering the life of the local church. The ordained are the ones who call God's people to worship and prayer. They bear the responsibility of teaching the truths of our faith. They offer guidance in living a virtuous and moral life. The ordained have been referred to as those who have been taken away from worldly things so that they can devote their lives to the things of God. What do the activities associated with holy orders have to do with the life of ordinary families?

The connection becomes clearer when we focus on the idea of *ordering* the life of the community. Think of "ordering" in the sense of making arrangements, planning, negotiating, sorting and so forth. Then think of how much families need this.

Most of us fail to notice how much "ordering of the day" takes place in a typical family. Between getting up and going to bed, there are probably a hundred little events that require some planning and arranging. Think of all that goes into making sure that everyone in the family eats that day. Think about the effort involved in getting family members to where they have to go. Think of what's involved in planning a weekend. If we add up all these ordering actions in the church of the home, then we might begin to appreciate how much the life of the family requires holy ordering.

More than once I have complained (mostly in private) about how much our children need to be taken here and there for various activities. A good amount of our daily driving is to school, to athletic practices, to music lessons, to doctors' appointments, or to a friend's house. More than once I've asked myself, "Doesn't anyone ever walk anymore?"

Maybe if I were able to see that driving our children to music lessons or ball practice is really part of the work for which I was "ordained" as a parent, it would be a more meaningful experience. Then I might more easily see that I am helping to introduce my children to the beauty of music and to the exciting world of athletics. All of this may lead them to see and hear the echo of God's music in human song, to feel the joy of God's energy in running after a soccer ball. Then I may even enjoy the drive. Maybe. Miracles sometimes happen!

But, joking aside, I believe there is an authentic sacramental connection between what happens in the family and holy orders. Certainly, this correlation can be seen around the family's religious activities as well: the leading of meal prayers, the spontaneous "Amen" that arises when a child finishes a chore ahead of time, the family praying before leaving on a vacation trip—these are family holy orders at play.

When we think about it, there are many examples when a call to prayer, or more broadly speaking, an ordering of the chaos of everyday life, is accomplished by the cooperative work between a powerful God and a frazzled parent. These are sacramental times.

Love Creating Life

The Sacrament of Matrimony is a great symbol of God's creative love. God's love is expressed throughout the life of creation, and especially in those made in the divine image. God loved each of us and we came into being. There is no more basic spiritual principle in the universe. And it's at the heart of marital life too. I would join some of my theological colleagues in saying that Christian marriage is perhaps the most basic of all the sacraments of the church. It expresses in created act and social life what's at the core of creation.

But in saying that, I don't want to idealize this important reality with over-the-top romanticism or imply that marriage is all lovey-dovey. Sometimes marriage is simply hard work. Sometimes it's boring. There are days when not a few wives or husbands want to jump in the car by themselves and head for the setting sun.

Because marriage is always between two unique persons, it follows that the same can be said of their marriage: Each marriage is unique. Over the years, I have become an observer of the marriages of others and often wonder how so many pretty strange people find each other and then marry—a peculiar him and an eccentric her, bound together in holy wedlock.

So what is this thing called marital love? And what makes it into a symbol of God's love for us? Start with the idea of differences. There is nothing more different than God and us: God always was, and we have not always been; God created the whole universe (perhaps many of them), and we are lucky if we can get our check book to balance; God is the source of all life, and we are merely its receivers. The differences are infinite, yet God loves us and we are all invited to return God's love.

Then there are the differences between men and women: Our brains operate differently; our reactions to virtually everything vary by gender. Yet couples can transcend those differences, leap across the chasm between them, and truly share their lives with each other. And this happens not just for a day but for a lifetime.

There are those who decry the seemingly high rate of divorce in our society. But I sometimes think that given the freedom in our world, given the differences between men and women, given the capability of both genders to survive independently, it's a wonder (and a bit miraculous) how *any* marriage lasts for a lifetime. Yet many, many do. Married love continues despite the odds and in spite of the times when it is strained to the limit.

We all have our marital war stories. My wife and I have known moments when we've had to survive one storm or another. We have grown to accept each other's eccentricities and learned adaptive strategies as we try to stay together.

A simple example. My wife enjoys combining physical exercise (mostly walking) with intensive shopping. This is not my interest. Therefore, when we shop together, I can feel our relationship entering a potential storm. As soon as we enter a store, she's off and running. I, on the other hand, seek out the one object we have come to buy in order to capture it. She decides to look for any of a thousand items we *might* buy, especially if they are on sale. Almost every time we shop, I lose contact with her. She somehow disappears behind counters piled high with clearance merchandise. I'm ready to exit when she is just warming up.

My strategy now is to find something else to do. Fortunately, in the part of town where she likes to shop, there are a couple of good bookstores. While she explores the clearance racks, I sit and read. I support her shopping adventure, but at a safe distance. She applauds my interest in books. Marriages that survive have learned how to make similar arrangements in almost every area of life together. There's a give-and-take,

At the heart of family life is the presence of a love that is practical, generous and down-to-earth.

a pervasive calculus that keeps the life of wife and husband balanced and connected.

That's what it's like with God and us. God respects our humanity, and we respect God's divinity. We are gifted with freedom to pursue our lives as best we can, although we also try to do what God wants of us. In a sense, we and God give each other space, while remaining close. A good marriage embodies the same reciprocity.

Marital love includes the other's best interests. It is not possessive or controlling. It does not turn the other into anyone less than a full equal in all things. It literally and fully applies the description of love found in the First Corinthians, the thirteenth chapter, a passage often read at weddings.

Part of the love between wife and husband are those special expressions of sexual intimacy that can bring forth new life. The generative love expressed in the marital act is continued in hundreds of ways. At the heart of family life is the presence of a love that is practical, generous and down-to-earth. At its core, family spirituality is essentially relational.

All genuine interpersonal love is sacred. Wherever love happens, God is there in its midst. But some human love is more intense, more total, and more encompassing than others. It involves one's total self: body, spirit and soul. When that kind of love is present, God dances with joy. Sacred are those moments when this happens in ordinary families.

The Way Home

For some, the best road to heaven
would be a super-highway,
straight and smooth.
Put the car in cruise control
and let the destination appear
as soon as possible.

For me, I'll take the scenic route
with all sorts of side trips to unknown places.
I'd like to find an overlook or pull off every place
that promises something I've never ever seen.
Give me lots of ups and downs
like a roller coaster
with some scary parts too.

I want to remember not just getting there,
but every milepost and distraction along the way.
I don't mind detours either.
Make it exciting and an adventure.
Otherwise, I may grow old.

CHAPTER FOUR

Family Prayer

Family prayer has for its very own object
family life itself, which in all its varying circumstances
is seen as a call from God
and lived as a filial response to his call....
The dignity and responsibility of the Christian family
as a domestic church can be achieved only
with God's unceasing aid,
which sure will be granted
if it is humbly and trustingly
petitioned in prayer.

—John Paul II

For some people, the spiritual life seems far away, as if God were a distant king who lives atop a jagged ridge in a castle protected on all sides by a deep moat. A prayer from an ordinary person—even a *good* prayer—might not reach such a God. At best, if you wanted to make a petition, you would have to find an important person—a mediator, if you will—and ask that person to carry your prayer to the king. Then all you could do was hope your request eventually reached its destination.

But when we look at the life of Jesus, we see a different picture. He was a person of deep prayer, and his life unfolded through his constant awareness of God's presence. And when his disciples asked him to teach them how to pray, he gave them a great gift in a few words. He taught them a *family* prayer.

The familiar opening words, "Our Father," identify immediately that we are part of God's family. We are to pray to God not as *the* God, or *my* God or even *Jesus'* God, but as *our* God. This means we are never alone. Even when we pray in private, we are invited to use the language of familiarity, the language of family.

How we pray says a lot about who we are. Prayer is a window for seeing, deep down, what is really important to us. Each family harbors its own spirit, and its identity feeds off that spirit, whatever it is, every day. When the family spirit reflects the presence of God's Holy Spirit, the family spirit finds expression in the prayer life of the family. Prayer signals where we put our faith and trust.

This is critical for families, because when there is a lot of uncertainty in family life, faith and trust go a long way in helping families survive. When faith and trust in God accompany the family on its precarious journey through life, prayer can be a powerful survival skill.

I use the word *survival* in its most expansive meaning—not as an indicator of minimal life but as a sign of life in abundance. Prayer connects us with the source of the fullness of life. We can call upon God and that's exactly what God wants us to do. Knock at the door, ring my bell, says God, even in the midst of your worst day. No, *especially* on those days. Prayer is not for the weak, but for those who know the source of genuine strength.

Preparing the Ground

When John Paul II wrote about learning to pray, he did not call parents to begin by teaching their children specific prayers. Instead, he urged parents to introduce children "to gradual discovery of the mystery of God and to personal dialogue with him."

There is much to think about here. He is suggesting an *attitude* about prayer that is rooted in a sense of God's mystery immediately around us. This is especially important for young children. Those who study the spirituality of children describe them as "natural mystics." By respecting and seeking to develop this natural sense of spirituality in children, we help them acknowledge God's ingenious way of creating life and encourage their openness to life in all its forms.

Natural Mystics

I once heard a parent say that one of the best ways to introduce children to prayer was to take them to a cathedral or beautiful church when it is empty. The kids will instinctively know what to do, she insisted. There is considerable merit in this suggestion. Children have a natural sense of wonder. And what is more wonderful to a child than an immensely cavernous room that is different from every other place her or she knows? While it doesn't have to be a magnificent cathedral, take your child to the most awesome church you can find. This gesture is an open invitation to connect the child's imagination with the idea of God in a wondrous setting. Let the Holy Spirit do the rest. Allow the child to soak in the whole scene. Don't rush in one door and out the other. Don't interpret. Allow what's there to make the impression.

I had the good fortune of growing up in a Catholic parish that had a church that was truly awe-inspiring. The pastor was of German background, and he brought to this parish a great sense of architectural beauty. For liturgical purists, the interior of the church was probably horrid. It was a mix of Italian renaissance and baroque ornamentation, and sprinkled about the church were very realistic-looking statues of practically every canonized saint up to 1950. The Stations of the Cross were life-size and totally realistic, at least to the eyes of a six-year-old.

The whole place was illumined by thousands of lights, most of which were hidden from sight by gold gilt ornamentation. High atop the main altar (imported Italian white marble) was a painted mural that followed the curved vaulted ceiling. It must have been a hundred feet long! In its center was a scene depicting the Holy Family on an average day in Nazareth. On one side was a painting of the pastor seated with various architects and construction engineers discussing the original building of the church. On the other side was an equally impressive picture of the church being constructed with large, smoke-belching factories in the background. (The church was located in the industrial corridor of northwest Indiana.) That I am still able to picture in great detail the look of this church suggests to me the power of a church to inscribe a sense of wonder and mystery in the mind of a child. My memories of this church remain part of the awe I feel whenever I think of God.

Awesome Wonders

"Seeing is believing." There is nothing more powerful than the visual in helping children form their ideas of God. Therefore, my second suggestion for "teaching" children about prayer is to escort them into the wonders of God's creation in nature. And, as in the church, let the Spirit of God do the rest.

Especially with young children, exposure to nature is one of the best ways to teach them about ways to pray to God. The natural world demonstrates God's power, beauty, magnanimity, and most of all God's availability—a great foundation for a wondrous and positive image of God.

It is interesting to note that in a study by the American Camp Association of kids who went to summer camp—whether a religious camp

The natural world demonstrates God's power, beauty, magnanimity, and most of all God's availability—a great foundation for a wondrous and positive image of God.

or not, whether their parents were believers or atheists—there was a statistically significant increase in children's spirituality levels after they attended camp. Apparently, just getting the kids outdoors makes them appreciate nature and think about who created it.

Our family has always enjoyed taking vacations together. Especially when our children were young, my wife and I wanted to show them the wonders of the created universe—at least those close to the highway. We constantly kept an eye out for that spectacular overlook or scenic route that would show a particular instance of God's artistic handiwork. After we came home, we would continue to talk about our trips (even the typical comedies and unplanned emergencies) and enjoy our slides. My guess is that these trips were an important part of the religious and spiritual development of our children, preparing the ground for what would develop in later years.

Humble Examples

"Preparing the ground." That's an important general principle to remember in all of our religious education of our children. As parents, we are always preparing our children for what's ahead. And in that sense, the teaching of basic attitudes, beliefs and values is more important than any specific words.

While others will later help our children put up the "walls" and build the "roof," we parents are the ones who lay down the foundation. That foundation establishes a solid base for the rest of their lives. In fact, their "house" won't stand against the winds that are forecast for the future without the strong underpinnings we establish at home.

With this in mind, I want to share a moment in my own upbringing that made one of the deepest impressions on me about prayer. (I was a quite impressionable eleven-year-old at the time.) Our family had the custom of praying the family rosary, but there were times when my father would "pass" on joining my mom, my sisters and I in our evening ritual. While we assembled in one of the bedrooms to pray, he would stay in the living room. At the time, I was concerned, but now, many years later, I have a new perspective on Dad's decision to stay in the living room by himself. Back then, I had little insight into the personal needs of a parent. (What child does?) Now, as a husband, parent of seven, and working educator and writer, I suspect that he just needed some "space," some alone time to shake off the burdens and worries of a busy day. He wasn't anti-family, anti-prayer or anti-rosary. He just needed some precious moments to relax and, for all I know, pray that he would have the strength to keep going.

But one night I walked into my parents' bedroom near the end of the day and found my father kneeling beside the bed. As the saying goes, you could have knocked me over with a feather. I was shocked. Here was my dad, not a very religious person on the outside, kneeling before the Lord of the Universe, the God of creation and redemption. In my mind back then, my father was virtually omnipotent. He was a successful businessman, an accomplished athlete and a professional golfer. He was a man of strength. But there he was, kneeling. It was one of the greatest lessons I ever learned about praying. It was at least as much as I learned in eight years as a vowed religious. It outdistanced, I am sure, as much as I learned about prayer as a professional theologian.

To use John Paul II's words, "The concrete example and living witness of parents is fundamental and irreplaceable in educating their children to prayer."

Amen, I say, amen.

The Heart of Family Spirituality

Research across religions shows that mealtimes are the most customary setting for family prayer, with bedtime prayers coming in a close second. Each night at bedtime, I would say prayers with our younger children, and part of our routine was to recite a litany of prayers for each family member. Often the prayers would include some expression of contrition for the sins we might have committed that day. We would also name others whom we wanted to remember.

As simple as this bedtime ritual might seem, I believe daily prayers together are a meaningful way to hold the family together. I also know that prayer can stir us to responsible actions that support what we request in our prayers.

If we take a second look at our common mealtime and bedtime prayers, we can see that they are at least loosely associated with life and death. Meals sustain our lives. Because sleep includes a loss of consciousness and a loss of control over one's situation, bedtime prayers remind us that our very lives are in God's loving hands. (I suspect that there is not a parent alive who has not at least once thought about the possibility of SIDS while tucking in an infant before sleep.) Prayer draws life into perspective. That is one of the great values of praying. It brings us before God, who is both the source of life and the power that keeps it going.

Outside the home, prayer continues to bring the family together. When we gather to celebrate sacramental family moments, such as bap-

Blessings are a wonderful family ritual, easily done. They express the heart of family spirituality by bringing God's love and protection down to earth.

tisms, confirmations and weddings, prayer is a significant component. For me, the marriages of our older children—and the baptisms of their children—were major spiritual moments in my life.

Another longstanding tradition in families is the practice of blessing children. I think it is one of the most underused, and potentially one of the best, of all family rituals. Typically, parents might bless children before bedtime, or blessings might accompany a shared meal. Being Catholic, our family used the sign of the cross at the beginning of the meal prayer. Even now when we gather with our older children and their spouses, who are not Catholic, we often use this seemingly "Catholic" gesture.

A blessing is any intentional ritual that acknowledges God's presence and the sacredness of who or what is being blessed. Signing a person with a cross is but one way to do this; blessings transcend all religious differences. I can think of many wonderful prayers and blessings from other religious traditions, specifically, some quite moving prayers from the Jewish and Muslim traditions.

Blessing children as they leave the home can be especially touching. I have noticed that this practice is particularly important for Hispanic Christians. Wishing them well and requesting God's guidance and protection can be done in a thousand different ways. In brief, it's always some way of saying to our children, "*Vaya con Dios*, go with God. We love you, and so does God."

Blessings are a wonderful family ritual, easily done. They express the heart of family spirituality by bringing God's love and protection down to earth. How fitting it is for parents to bless their children. And for the children to bless their parents. It is a meaningful reminder that life is a precious gift from God.

The Crisis of Limits

There are times when all we can do is pray for our family. As a spouse and parent, I know there is a limit to what I can do for my wife and children, so I augment my limited effort with prayer for them. Over the years, I have remained connected with my family by thought, word, deed and prayer. I pray because it keeps me close to my loved ones, even when the miles separate us.

I have also found a deep need to pray for myself. They used to say that middle age brings us to face "the crisis of limits." Being on the far side of middle age, I now nod in full agreement to this view. I know all too well that I am sorely limited in strength and courage to do all that is necessary to be a good spouse, parent and person.

Earlier in my life I had picked up the idea that love of oneself and attention to one's own needs was at odds with loving others. I had concluded that my needs were supposed to be the last ones considered in the family. It was sanctifying, I thought, to volunteer to be a suffering servant. In fact, I believed that I would be blessed for my self-denial.

I cannot say that I was ruined by this "others first, me last" philosophy. But I know now that I can be a better husband and father if I take care of myself and say "no" sometimes—especially if I am tired and worn down by the day's challenges. I am not saying that I come first, but I need to balance a consideration of my own needs with those of the rest of our family. Then, in a sense, everyone wins. So I pray for myself that I may have the wisdom to make good decisions for the good of all of us.

I think of the many times Jesus slipped away to a quiet place to rest and pray when he felt overwhelmed by the demands and pressures from the crowds. My own father would often do the same. I have learned to do something like that. When I am feeling overwhelmed, I look to see if Jesus might be around for a little conversation about how things are going for both of us. He and I enjoy those moments together.

Late-Night Conversation

Me:

Dear God,
It's quiet outside but not inside me.
The day wore me down
almost to ground level.

Once again, I know that alone
I cannot do it.

At times I was not even there,
so filled was I with worry and fear
that I even missed my child's smile.

The money, yes the money we don't have,
and that uncertain future I so easily imagine
is the worst.

I just don't know if we make it.

God:

I will guide you into the difficult open space
to help you stretch and grow,
becoming someone who loves with fierce intent,
fully in the mix of all life's ups and downs.

I want you to run into the fire, not away from it.
I want others,
especially your children,
to find in you
what I hope you find in me—
a love that can cry when it's good,
and laugh when it's not.

Rest now
in my love for you.

CHAPTER FIVE

The School of Love

By virtue of their ministry of educating,
parents are through the witness of their lives
the first heralds of the Gospel for their children.
Furthermore, by praying with their children,
by reading the word of God with them
and by introducing them deeply
through Christian initiation into the body of Christ
—both the eucharistic and the ecclesial body—
they become fully parents,
in that they are begetters not only of bodily life
but also of the life
that through the Spirit's renewal
flows from the cross and resurrection of Christ.

—John Paul II

In matters of love, sending cards and letters are fine. So are gifts, especially if the gift-giver personally creates them. But when all is said and done, appearing *in person* best says, "I love you."

And that's exactly what God did. No signs and wonders, no fireworks in the sky. Just simple presence in our midst. God's most important act, after creating the universe, was taking flesh in the person of Jesus Christ. How could anything be more telling? In Jesus, God's personal love for us became physically present and real. Just so, the heart of the spiritual life of the family lies in this central message: Be present to those you love, a witness to God's love for all; *live* your love.

When it comes to lifelong influence, those who express their beliefs and values with their lives are the ones who shape and inspire us. Some people try to convince us by words and contrived actions. While that may work at least for a time, it eventually evaporates like rain on a hot sidewalk. We are touched and changed primarily by those whom we sense are real and authentic.

Look at how many ways we emphasize the importance of being authentic: "Walk the talk." "Put your money where your mouth is," "Tell it like it is," or, as one of my favorites lines from the musical *My Fair Lady* puts it, "Love, love, love, love. You said that you love me. *Show* me!"

Remember the Apostle Thomas? He was one of the "chosen," one of the twelve who had walked, talked and eaten with Jesus, witnessing his miracles. Thomas had every chance to hear and believe Jesus' message. Yet after Jesus' resurrection, even though the other disciples told Thomas they had seen Jesus, he responded, "Unless I see the mark of the nails in his hands, and put my finger in the mark of the nails and my hand in his side, I will not believe" (John 20:25). In other words, "*Show* me!" It wasn't until Jesus appeared in person to Thomas and said, "Put your finger here and see my hands. Reach out your hand and put it in my side. Do not doubt." (John 20:27), that Thomas could believe.

Jesus knew the importance of being present and real. As his earthly life came to an end, he needed a way for his presence to continue. He called his followers to become *the body of Christ,* to carry Jesus from the hills and valleys of Palestine and ultimately across land and sea to the ends of the earth.

The first apostles were sent with the Gospel in their hearts to inform others of the wondrous presence of God in the life, death and resurrection of Jesus. They were evangelists—Gospel communicators. In fact, the Latin word for "gospel" is *evangelium.* Just as the Word of God was personified in the life of Jesus, the apostles were to communicate *through their lives* the substance of what Jesus taught.

The important message for us is that being a witness to God's loving word is not something that comes from title or role or position or status. There is no such thing as an official or designated witness. Evangelization is not the task of an elite few, in a scheduled time or specific place. It is not the work of manipulative pressure or slick advertising. It is rooted in the honest expression of a Christian life that is lived and shared. It means being a walking witness to God's love 24/7.

To live out the compassion and hospitality of Jesus, to love as he did, is the essence of the Christian life. While this can take place wherever we go, within the family is a special place, a privileged place, for this process of evangelization to happen. For most of us, that's where our Christianity begins. Some would say it begins before we are even born.

Living Faith

If I asked a typical family how they evangelize, I would probably be greeted with a blank stare. And there are good reasons for this reaction. Many people see the communication of Christian faith as the role of formal religious education, a place where parents bring their children and let the "professionals" do their work. While a family might engage in some religious activities, they might not perceive what they do to be as important as what takes place in the church. In fact, many view the home as the place that people *leave* to go to church.

The truth is that parents are primary evangelists but rarely think of themselves that way. And even if they do, many confess that they don't do a very good job of it. So we need to start by affirming the central role of family evangelization. Then we need to deepen our appreciation of the family's role in deepening the life of faith.

For many years I have been involved in preparing young children for the sacraments of Reconciliation and First Eucharist, and I always follow the practice of including both children and their parents in my classes. Every year, some cannot understand why I want the parents in the classroom. At the first class, I can read the faces of those who wanted to be somewhere else. But eventually they come to appreciate that the spiritual lives of their children are deeply connected to and influenced by the life of the whole family.

It always takes a bit of gentle convincing for parents to grasp the full import of this idea. Some of the problem comes from their assumption that if they were expected to "evangelize" they would be expected to *teach* the various truths of the Christian faith to their children. Many were uncomfortable with doing that, fearing they might "get it wrong" or feeling uneasy about their own doubts. I would often startle them by suggesting that their role was, in some ways, harder than teaching the faith: They were supposed to *live* it. That was their primary task as Christian parents.

So, what does it mean to live your faith? Here are some ideas of what "evangelization" might look like in your daily family life:

- Treat your children with respect and kindness.
- Bring God into your family conversation when it seems appropriate.
- Share with your children your own worries and hopes.
- Speak well of other people.
- Take interest in the world of your children.
- Speak of death and Christian hope.
- Work alongside your children in doing some of the family's chores.

The heart of evangelization is to imitate the spiritual orientation of Jesus: to love God and neighbor with your whole heart.

- Express love and affection for your children.
- Pray together as a family.
- Find meaningful ways to help the needy of the world.
- Monitor and talk about what's being offered by the media.
- Care for your pets and property.
- Joyfully attend church events.
- Take time to have fun with each other.
- Keep connected with family members who live at a distance.
- Merrily celebrate birthdays and other important anniversaries.
- Notice if anyone in the family feels down or sad.
- Share food at any time of the day or night.

As you look at this list, I hope you get the point that these are not "extras" that you have to add to your schedule but rather a living expression of the ways of Jesus. When I picture the disciples after that first Pentecost, I don't see them so much "preaching" Jesus as "sharing" Jesus. Because it was a Jewish feast day, the city was crowded, and I think the disciples simply *mingled* among those who were there that day in Jerusalem. They didn't use microphones or shout from the housetops. They just went out and shared what was most important to them. As parents, we can do exactly the same with our children. My experience, however, convinces me that most of us need encouragement to do so...and maybe a little guidance.

The heart of evangelization is to imitate the spiritual orientation of Jesus: to love God and neighbor with your whole heart. In family terms that means first loving your spouse and your children, day after day, through thick and thin.

The Power—and Pressure—of Parenthood

A young girl of three was standing with her dad on a bluff overlooking the Pacific Ocean. It was that wonderful time of the day, just before sunset, and they had come to that spot to watch the blazing sun fall gently into the sea. Soon, the sun was touching the top edge of the distant water. As it slipped beneath the surface, the father slowly raised his hand. Exactly mimicking the disappearing sun, he lowered his hand while solemnly saying, "Going, going, *gone*!"

The child stood in amazement, for precisely when her dad said, "*Gone*," the sun disappeared. Looking out over the water again and then looking back up to her dad, she said, "Daddy, do it again!"

This story speaks to the assumed incredible power of the parent in the eyes of a small child. For the child, the parent is like a god who rules the day and night. Eventually, this belief will wither away, but for a while it is part of what constitutes the world for a young developing mind. In the beginning, the world comes into the child almost entirely through the parent. That was God's intent. It was a brilliant idea.

Today, however, a lot is said about the negative influence of parents on their children, especially during their early years. So many individuals, it seems, enter adulthood with deep wounds that come from parental acts of abuse and neglect. Children come into the world hungry for acceptance and affirmation—tons of both—but parents sometimes fail to adequately nourish them. The parent "god" fails to deliver the goods.

There is a widespread tendency to scapegoat parents for the evils of society. The penal system does it. So do the schools. This is unfortunate, because if anyone needs a supportive environment it is a parent. The work of being a "good enough" parent is demanding and at times unrewarding, unless parents have a good overall sense of their value. The time required for effective parenting competes with work time all too often. So many parents are stressed, worried, confused and tired—all at the same time.

We would do well to remember John Paul II's description of parental love, that it "is irreplaceable and inalienable and therefore incapable of being entirely delegated to others or usurped by others." Family life is like the basic cell life of the human body. When it is healthy and doing its job, so to speak, the rest of the body will survive. When it's not, the ill effects are almost without number.

The time is ripe for a new awareness and appreciation of the role that family plays in human development, especially during the early years. Parenting is the best investment we can make for the future, the most important thing we ever do. Our effort is worth it.

I have a little reminder of this on a card in my office that says one-hundred years from now it will not matter how much I owned or where I had traveled or how many books I had written, but what really will matter is whether or not I was "big" in the life of a child. In other words, that I made a difference in the quality of another person's life. And you know what? Countless parents do just that. My hope is that some day, they will sit down in an easy chair after a long hard day, take a deep breath, and know this in all its magnificent detail.

A Natural Learning Environment

We as parents have incredible power. But there is another side to this coin: With power comes responsibility. As parents, we are responsible for the mental, emotional, and spiritual education of our children. We are positioned to be their first educators. I'm not talking about education as formal instruction, but as a process of formation or influence.

Pope John Paul II described the Christian family as a "school of love." During a homily on the feast of St. Joseph, he offered the following reflection: "We see then how the family must be *the first school of love and solidarity*, the first school of all the human and Christian virtues. Great, then, is the responsibility of parents! The family is a *community of love* where every member feels understood, accepted and loved and seeks to understand, accept and love the others."

Clearly, what is learned in the family goes well beyond what can be learned from a textbook or even the greatest classroom teacher. And it is learned *first* by being loved. It is learned when one feels valued and cared for by someone of tremendous importance in one's life.

In the lexicon of church life, *family catechesis* is the term used to describe the religious instruction that parents provide for their children. Professional catechists know that their influence on their children is quite limited. They know that it is much better when the classroom discussion is reinforced at home by how life is lived in the home. The home is the natural learning environment of the child, especially if we think of education as *learning to live*.

Further, there is a growing appreciation of the home as a sacred setting, a place where God's Spirit is both present and active. Not only is religious development a lifelong process (parents need to continue learning about their faith too), but teaching is most effective when learners are in the process of actively questioning. As a teacher, I can tell when the answer I am giving is not connected with any question currently inhabiting the minds of my students. Their response is, basically, "the blank stare."

What's called in educational circles "a teachable moment" is that time when a live question is on the table. That's when a student listens with all ears. That's when it's best to teach. And those moments happen for children mostly at home. So it makes sense that the family "school of love" is the most influential school of Christian faith.

Suppose a child asks, "Why did Grandma have to die?" Parents can be right there with a response that flows from their understanding of these matters. And parents have an opportunity, too, to recognize those moments when a child has a question that is not surfacing. Answers to questions that a child is afraid to ask are the best answers of all.

Like evangelization, family catechesis is not limited to a time or

Family catechesis flows from the real life and love of the family—the kind of love that allows us to share our time and energy with others, to give the gift of ourselves in serving others' needs.

place. It is not limited to written or verbal instruction. Like evangelization, it flows from the real life and love of the family—the kind of love that allows us to share our time and energy with others, to give the gift of ourselves in serving others' needs. When children see this process of faith in their parents' actions, their own reception of faith, is even more intensified.

For example, my mother's actions certainly had this effect on my appreciation of a vibrant Christian faith. When I was about ten, I volunteered to become an altar boy. This role was not that special, because virtually all the boys in our class did the same. Each morning there were five masses celebrated in our parish: three in the basement of the church, one in the big church upstairs that was attended by five hundred half-awake children, and one very early mass in the hospital chapel. For reasons I cannot remember now, I told the sister who assigned the altar boys that I would like to serve the hospital mass. It was at six a.m. That meant I had to catch the city bus at five-thirty in morning. So there I would be standing next to men who worked at the local steel mills and oil refineries, waiting in the cold for the bus.

My mother must have taken pity on me and decided that she would drive me to the early mass. There was only one problem: She didn't know how to drive. So on her own she took lessons, got her license, and soon I no longer had to wait for the bus. I had my own chauffeur.

I'm sure that my mom did many generous acts of love for me. But her thoughtfulness in learning to drive just to be able to take me to mass stands out as special in my memory. It was love turned into selfless action. It became a part of my universe, wrapped in God's gracious love.

What's It All About?

As a parent myself, I have sometimes wondered whether it would be easier to be just a parent, without the additional demands of being a *Christian* parent. I feel the burden of being a "witness" when one of our children calls me to bring a drink of water in the middle of the night or when I would rather watch a good football game than go to a soccer practice of little girls. But then I step back—almost always—and ask myself the classic question from the movie *Alfie:* "What's it all about?"

Then I think about what I have learned from the church concerning what is really important. John Paul II frequently used two words in his writings on family life: *vocation* and *minister*. The first implies being called or invited by God to do some special work in building up God's kingdom here on earth. The second implies actually doing the work of God—as a sort of a stand-in for God.

John Paul II called the family a *community of love.* To live in community is no small challenge. What makes life easy or difficult, however, is often not related to the difficulty of the task or the challenges involved. What makes our lives bearable is the *meaning* we experience as we live together. A meaningless life is intolerable even on good days. But if we can appreciate that how we invest our time and energy with one another is worthwhile and has consequences far into the future, then almost anything can be done with joy.

Life offers us many options. For those who choose Christian family life with a generous spirit, their families become an earthly, sacramental expression of God's life lived on earth as it is in heaven. Celebrating life with strong love—that's the essence of God's plan as lived and taught by Jesus Christ.

The Whole World in My Hands

The soft feel of a baby's body
resting in my arms
is among life's great pleasures.

We parents know this moment
as well as that sacred reversal of sensations
when we feel held by the baby
in a wondrous ocean of warmth and comfort
as the whole universe holds us
in an embrace that will last forever.

CHAPTER SIX

The Domestic Church

At different times in the Church's history

and also in the Second Vatican Council,

the family has well deserved the beautiful name of

"the domestic Church."

This means there should be found in every Christian family

the various aspects of the entire church.

Furthermore, the family, like the Church,

ought to be a place where the Gospel is transmitted

and from which the Gospel radiates.

In a family which is conscious of its mission,

All the members evangelize and are evangelized.

The parents not only communicate the Gospel to their children,

but from their children

they can themselves receive the same Gospel as deeply lived by them.

—Paul VI

Calling the family "a domestic church" was first introduced in modern times at Vatican II. The phrase was used by Paul VI, John Paul I, and John Paul II. In fact, the times John Paul II referred to the Christian family as "the domestic church" would have to number in the hundreds or even thousands. He wanted families to know that *their* life is genuine church life. He wanted the whole church to acknowledge and reverence this dimension of church life. He believed that the love expressed and lived day after day was like the pebble dropped in the pond: Its ripples of influence spread into infinity.

But what really is this idea of "domestic church" and why is it so important? Does it mean that the Christian family *is* a real, bona fide, genuine church, or is this just a pietistic or poetic way of saying something nice about the family? Is the phrase intended to be understood as deeply *real,* or is it simply a metaphor?

There are some who argue against this idea of family as church, saying that the family should not want to be a part of an organization that already has too many problems of its own. Others feel that in keeping a little distance from the church the family can more easily thrive, because distance provides freedom. Some view it as being too idealistic and abstract. Others, including myself, find the phrase quite meaningful. It is a way of empowering family life, supporting a deeper, more meaningful freedom.

At a United States Bishops' Committee on Marriage and Family Life, one of the biggest drawbacks raised against the use of term was that it might imply that only *perfect* families could be real domestic churches. A comment made by one of the women participants was a particularly eloquent response. She said that her whole understanding of family life had been changed once she learned her family was a true church. "Before I became aware of this image," she said, "I didn't think of myself as a very holy person. Because of holding down a job and raising my three children as a single parent, I wasn't involved with my parish or any church ministry. But when I realized that in the loving, forgiving, sacrificing and getting through the hassles of everyday family living I was participating in the dying and rising of Jesus and extending his message and ministry into the world it gave me the motivation to do what God is calling me to do and helped me to realize that what I do in the family is very holy, very sacred."

In the end, the symposium published a set of conclusions supporting the family as "domestic church" for the following reasons:

- The concept of being "church" will help families see that their ordinary life in the family is sacred.
- Being "church" will alert families that they have a special mission to bring goodness, peace and justice into the world.
- Being "church" will encourage families to reflect on how their daily life connects with the overall work of God, begun with Jesus and continuing with his followers.

A Third Option

For the past few years, a rather heated debate has gone on between those who say that Jesus actually had a rather anti-family message and those who claim that Jesus was very pro-family as it was lived in his time. I have come to believe that there is a third option, one that arises from what Paul terms "the New Creation."

Family life in the time of Jesus was, for the most part, an unjust social system. Households were ruled by the patriarch in residence. Women and children were listed with the man's possessions, and his rule was virtually absolute. A husband, for example, was allowed to divorce his wife if she were a poor cook!

Those who note that Jesus had a certain anti-family message are right. Jesus could not accept or affirm family life as he saw it practiced in his culture. He saw the harm and hurt of the systems of male domination around him. He had to reject the patriarchal system because it did not affirm the family as a community of persons with all members being equal and deserving of respect.

Jesus advocated another way. His prophetic gesture of washing the feet of his disciples said it all: You call me Lord, and right you are; this is how a good Lord acts; take off your sandals and get ready for the soap and water.

There was also, in the cumulative message of Jesus, an invitation to lifelong celibacy. That seems to be Paul's advice, especially given his assumption that the end of the world was about to happen. Because the old structures of marriage and family life did not change overnight, a sort of gradual conversion was suggested to those who remained in those social arrangements. They were given modest encouragement and told to make the best of their lives in accord with Christian principles. Husbands and fathers were "in charge" and taught that they should lead with love, not power. Wives were told to respect their husbands. Children were asked to do the same for their parents.

But a glimmer of a third option for family life can be found in the New Testament around the concern for the care for widows and orphans. Scholars tell us their plight directly related to an unsavory side of the old patriarchal order. Back then, when a woman married she automatically became part of her husband's family. If he died, she was expelled from his family—but she and her children were not taken back into her original family. They were totally on their own. Exiled in a sense, they attempted survival without economic support and social connections of any sort.

The early Christian community recognized this unfortunate situation as a special calling to embody God's care for the marginalized. Special effort was made to incorporate widows and their families into Christian families. Caring for widows and orphans became a special sign of the generosity of the church as it was called into being a community of acceptance, forgiveness and compassion. Christian families were to be reconfigured according to the beliefs and values of Jesus. They were to become "family churches" in the New Creation, to be open to outsiders, to care for those in need, to be a community of equals. They were to recognize that people come from different backgrounds, enjoy different gifts from God, and exercise different roles in the life of the community. Finally, they were to recognize each other as equal in dignity and importance. No discrimination based on gender, social status or ethnic background was to be allowed.

Jesus also advocated full affirmation of the personhood of children. When, on at least one occasion, the disciples sought to put children back in their place, Jesus countered their effort by inviting children to come closer to him. Later, he used children as examples of those who more fully understood the nature of God's kingdom.

Christian families were to become "family churches" in the New Creation, to be open to outsiders, to care for those in need, to be a community of equals.

Being human, many Christians struggled with these ideals in the beginning. After all, they were only turning the entire existing society—with its strongly entrenched social beliefs and values—upside down. Yet this task had a telling effect on all societal relationships and stood as a revolutionary challenge for families of the early church. Their society was built on powerful barriers between those on the inside and those on the outside, those in power and those without power, Jew against Gentile, rich against poor, free person against slave, and men against women. Many of these differences touched the family. In the time of Jesus, people were often kept in their places by violent means. If a woman stepped out of place, she could be stoned. If a child stepped out of place, he or she could be whipped.

But this had to change. Jesus rejected these practices, and the early church received and applied his nonviolent approach. Jesus saw families as genuine communities of persons that were to affirm the full personhood and equality of all members, especially women and children. Historians note that there were an unusual number of women, children and slaves in the early church. We can understand why.

The quest for full equality is not easy when the grain of society goes otherwise. Even today, the practice of full equality between wives and husbands remains one of the greatest challenges within marriage. John Paul II wrote, "Inspired and sustained by the new commandment of love, the Christian family welcomes, respects and serves every human being, considering each one in his or her own dignity a person and as a child of

God." These words describe a genuine community of persons. There is no talk of headship. No talk of blind obedience. What is described is an interpersonal dynamic that can occur only between equals.

This interpersonal dynamic of equals, where love exists across, through, and in spite of differences, is the core of the New Creation. Literally, every individual act of genuine love and kindness, however small, makes a difference, right now and forever. Yet not a day passes where our love is not challenged. Opportunities to respond with love to each other in the family come toward us like a swiftly flowing stream: "Can you take me to band practice? Can I have my allowance early? Can I stay out late?" Our responses can, in a small but quite real way, embody God's love, the same love that "flared forth," as the scientist-priest Thomas Barry described the Universe at its very beginning.

The Christian family is a primary symbol of God's love made real. Family love is often ordinary and does not make headlines. Yet it embodies the central message of Jesus, not in a churchy kind of way but, as they say in some places, in a "down-home way." Because of this the Christian family can and deserves to be called the domestic church, the church of the home.

"You're in Church!"

One of the dangers of naming the family "the domestic church" is that some families may feel this designation excludes them because their family life is far from perfect. There are arguments and discord. Sometimes family members drop out into silence, or even move out. In most families there are occasional disagreements and frazzled nerves. Household projects sit for weeks unattended and atrophying. Sometimes individual family members—an underappreciated wife or mom, an overworked husband or dad, or an ignored and unseen child—just want to exit the whole scene. Sometimes they all want to head for the far corners of the universe for some peace and quiet.

Recognize any of this? All of it? Welcome to family life as it is really lived. And we want to call this *church?* Absolutely.

Think for a minute about the characters that made up the first Christian church. Think of their esteemed leaders, Peter and Paul. Peter was a major project for Jesus. He was continuously misunderstanding the basic drift of his teachings. And when he was given an opportunity to stand up and be counted as one of the followers of Jesus, he turned and ran. If Jesus had held job interviews for disciples, Peter probably would not have made it past the first cut. Nevertheless, Peter was put in charge.

Paul was no better. He burned with a short fuse, and when given the opportunity he fought directly against the followers of Jesus. He joined the effort to exterminate them. Nevertheless, he too was chosen. In a sense, he was put in charge of the expansion of the church. It's interesting that Paul talked about the foolishness inherent in the way of life that Jesus espoused. Perhaps he was thinking about his own foolishness and what God had done with that. Paul also wrote about how God worked with human weakness, almost saying that the weaker we are the easier it is for

God to really produce outstanding results.

Christianity is filled with paradoxes and irony. The world moves things one way, while God sometimes moves in the opposite direction. Sometimes what the world holds as success God sees as failure. Or what the world considers an ending is a beginning in God's eyes.

With this in mind, how do you think God might see ordinary, messy, disorganized, struggling, confused families? Do you think God would exit the home where toys were scattered all over the floor or last night's dishes were still around the kitchen sink or people were communicating with each other at a decibel reading akin to a jet engine taking off? Do you think God would avoid families that are hurting and struggling?

I think the answer to all these situations is obvious: *God is at home in every kind of family.* God is much more concerned about open and loving hearts than messes and clutter. When it comes to families, cleanliness is not next to godliness. Family is the most likely place in the world to have a heart broken. So it's a wonderful place for God the healer to be. As Jesus once said, he came more for the sick than for the healthy. Welcome, Jesus, to today's families. Enjoy the visit, and remember: "You're in church!"

The Future of the Family

In thinking about the future of the church and the outlook for family life, there is enough evidence around to imagine that both entities are in their declining years. Church attendance is down. Many consider the teachings of the church passé, especially in matters dealing with marriage and family life. And with the publicized scandals relating to clergy abuse of children, the moral authority of the church seems to be compromised, diminished or ignored.

When it comes to marriage and the family, a similar kind of decline can be noted. The traditional family structure of a mom and dad with three children is now one of the least common family structures in our society. Many single parents raise children alone. Grandparents are the primary caregivers for over a million children in the United States. There are over a half-million children in foster care. Thousands of infants and children are waiting to be adopted. The number of children born out of wedlock continues to rise. While divorce statistics seem to have plateaued over the last decade, the level still remains quite high.

In other words, the picture for both church and family survival offers enough evidence to lead some forecasters to predict that a day may come when both church and families will be considered quaint historical oddities. We must ask, in all honesty, does family—whether we're referring to the human family or the ecclesial family—have much shelf life?

Here's where Christian hope comes into play. Hope is a greatly undervalued virtue. When Christians list the three great virtues—faith, hope and charity—the one that drifts to the bottom of the list is hope. God has invested mightily in creation and become an essential part of it through the Incarnation. God is on the side of church and family, no matter what its current state or composition. In fact, as I hope is evident by now, church and family are ultimately the same reality. This hope is surely seeded into the fertile soil of redeemed creation. To enter the transformation at the heart of the gospel, we have to risk. Or, to use the language of hope, we have to trust.

Genuine success in this endeavor is never obvious. But deep down, it is happening. That is the Christian promise. We are all invited to live deep down in the heart of reality, in the heart of challenge, in the heart of family—where God's Spirit is firing into fruition a New Creation.

Are We There Yet?

We could still see our front porch
as we left for Grandma's home
when the question
first floated forward
from somewhere in the back of the van.

"Are we there yet?"

Is it simply that the mind of a small child
can't calculate distance,
doesn't feel process,
will not admit there's a space
between start and finish?

Or do we all need more patience
or hope in accepting
life when not perfect
or family when not happy
or church when not holy?

Blessed are those who accept that
we're not there yet
and enjoy the ride.

Barton, Stephen C. *The Family in Theological Perspective*. Edinburgh, Scotland: T & T Clark, 1996.

Bourg, Frances Caffrey. *Where Two or Three and Gathered: Christian Families as Domestic Churches*. Notre Dame, IN: University of Notre Dame Press, 2004.

Boyer, Mark G. *Home is a Holy Place: Reflections, Prayers and Meditations Inspired by the Ordinary*. Skokie, IL: ACTA Publications, 1997.

Buber, Martin. *I and Thou*. New York, NY: Simon and Schuster, 1970.

Cahill, Lisa Sowel. *Family: A Christian Social Perspective*. Minneapolis, MN: Fortress Press, 2000.

Catholic Household Blessing and Prayers. Washington, DC: National Council of Catholic Bishops, 1989.

Chesto, Kathleen. *Exploring the New Family: Parents and their Young Adults in Transition*. Winona, MN: St. Mary's Press, 2001.

Chesto, Kathleen. *Family Prayer for Family Times: Traditions, Celebrations and Rituals*. New London, CT: Twenty-Third Publications, 1995.

Coffey, Kathy. *Experiencing God with Your Children*. New York, NY: The Crossroad Publishing Company, 1997.

Coles, Robert. *The Spiritual Life of Children*. Boston, MA: Houghton Miffin Company, 1990.

Finley, Kathleen. *Prayers for the Newly Married.* Skokie, IL: ACTA Publications, 2006.

Finley, Mitch, and Kathleen Finley. *Building Christian Families*. Allen, TX: Thomas More Press, 1996.

Foley, Gerald. *Family-Centered Church: A New Parish Model*. Kansas City, MO: Sheed and Ward, 1995.

Ferder, Fran, and John Haegle. *Tender Fires: The Spiritual Promise of Sexuality.* New York, NY: The Crossroad Publishing Company, 2003.

Freudenburg, Ben, and Rick Lawrence. *The Family Friendly Church.* Loveland, CO: Group Publishing, 1998.

Friedman, Edwin H. *Generation to Generation: Family Process in Church and Synagogue*. New York, NY, and London, England: The Guilford Press, 1985.

Garland, Diana. *Sacred Stories of Ordinary Families: Living the Faith in Daily Life*. San Francisco, CA: Jossey-Bass, 2003.

Hellerman, Joseph H. *The Ancient Church as Family*. Minneapolis, MN: Fortress Press, 2001.

Lawler, Michael G., *Family: American and Christian.* Chicago, IL: Loyola Press, 1998.

Lawler, Michael and William Roberts (eds), *Christian Marriage and Family: Contemporary Theological and Pastoral Perspectives.* Collegeville, MN: The Liturgical Press, 1996.

Livingston, Patricia H. *This Blessed Mess*. Notre Dame, IN: Sorin Books, 2000.

Looney, Thomas P. *Praying the Family Rosary.* Skokie, IL: ACTA Publications, 2006.

McGrath, Tom. *Meditations for Busy Parents.* Skokie, IL: ACTA Publications, 2002.

McGrath, Tom. *Raising Faith-Filled Kids.* Chicago, IL: Loyola Press, 2000.

O'Connell-Cahill, Catherine. *Moms@MySpiritualGrowth.com: Meditations and Cool Websites for Active Moms.* Skokie, IL: ACTA Publications, 2005.

O'Connor, Ann Lang. *The Twelve Unbreakable Principles of Parenting.* Skokie, IL: ACTA Publications, 2006.

Pennington, M. Basil. *Vatican II: We've Only Just Begun*. New York, NY:

The Crossroad Publishing Company, 1994.

Rahner, Karl. *The Practice of Faith: A Handbook of Contemporary Spirituality*. New York, NY: The Crossroad Publishing Company, 1986.

Schillebeeck, Edward. *The Church with a Human Face*. New York, NY: The Crossroad Publishing Company, 1985.

Reardon, Patrick T. *Love Never Fails: Spiritual Reflections for Dads of All Ages.* Skokie, IL: ACTA Publications, 1995.

Reardon, Patrick T. *Daily Meditations (with Scripture) for Busy Dads.* Skokie, IL: ACTA Publications, 2006.

Robertson, Patricia. *Daily Meditations (with Scripture) for Busy Moms: Tenth Anniversary Edition.* Skokie, IL: ACTA Publications, 2003.

Strommen, Merton P., and Richard A. Hardel. *Passing on the Faith: A Radical New Model for Youth and Family Ministry*. Winona, MN: St Mary's Press, 2000.

Thompson, Marjorie J. *Family the Forming Center: A Vision of the Role of Family in Spiritual Formation*. Nashville, TN: Upper Room Books, 1989.

Viets, Amy. *Making Faith Fun: 132 Spiritual Activities You Can Do with Your Kids.* Skokie, IL: ACTA Publications, 2006

Westerhoff, John H. *Will Our Children Have Faith?* (revised edition). Toronto, Ontario: Morehouse Publishing, 2000.

Wiederkehr, Macrina. *Gold in Your Memories: Sacred Moments, Glimpses of God.* Notre Dame, IN: Ave Maria Press, 1998.

Wigger, J. Bradley. *The Power of God at Home: Nurturing our Children in Love and Grace.* San Francisco, CA: Jossey-Bass, 2003.

Wright, Wendy M. *Seasons of a Family's Life: Cultivating the Contemplative Spirit at Home*. San Francisco, CA: Jossey-Bass, 2003.

With greater concern for family life spreading in both church and society in the 1970s and early 1980s, I felt strongly that there needed to be professional academic training for those wanting to dedicate their energy to helping families, especially in the setting of church. So in 1982 I created a graduate program in family ministry and adult religious education at Regis University in Denver, Colorado. For twenty years, that program brought together leading educators and students from around the world to explore ways to empower the great variety of families now part of church membership. I want to thank everyone involved in that program, for they contributed mightily to this book.

A special thanks as well to all those associated with Holy Cross Family Ministries, especially Father John Phalen, CSC, for their support of the research and writing that went into this book. They keep alive the vision of Father Patrick Peyton, CSC, who quite prophetically supported the family as a special place where God is present and active.

Finally, so much of what I know and value about family life comes from my own family, my wife, Karen, and our seven children—Sarah, Michael, Peter, Joseph, Timothy, Merrilee and Shanika. The same can be said for my family of origin, my mom and dad, Mary and Michael, along with my three sisters, Gail, Mary Jo, and Kathy.

Holy Cross Family Ministries is privileged to support Dave Thomas' work for families everywhere. *A Community of Love* is a wonderful spiritual tool to assist all families in their efforts to grow together in Christ and to become holy families. Our founder, Servant of God Father Patrick Peyton, CSC, believed and often said, "the family that prays together stays together." May families everywhere learn and pray together every day.

Headquartered in North Easton, Massachusetts, with offices in 16 countries worldwide, Holy Cross Family Ministries promotes family prayer to bring unity and peace to families. Founded in 1942 by Servant of God Father Patrick Peyton, CSC, candidate for sainthood, Holy Cross Family Ministries continues the mission of promoting daily family prayer, particularly the Rosary.

For more information on Holy Cross Family Ministries and its member ministries: Family Rosary, Family Theater Productions, Family Rosary International and Father Peyton Family Institute, go to www.hcfm.org, www.familytheater.org or call 800-299-PRAY.

"The family that prays together stays together."
Servant of God Father Patrick Peyton, CSC
1909-1992